D0045405

DOWNTON ABBEY

RULES FOR
HOUSEHOLD STAFF

CONTAINING THE MOST
APPROVED DIRECTIONS

AND GUIDANCE FOR STAFF IN
EVERY STATION WITHIN THE HOUSEHOLD IN
ORDER TO DISCHARGE THEIR DUTIES

CORRECTLY & WITH EFFICIENCY.

WITH
PARTICULAR INSTRUCTIONS
FOR THE:

BUTLER
HOUSEKEEPER
COOK
VALET
LADY'S MAID
FOOTMAN
HOUSEMAID
KITCHEN STAFF

AND INCLUDING
USEFUL INFORMATION

ON TRIED AND TESTED METHODS FOR ALL.

DOWNTON
ABBEY

RULES FOR
HOUSEHOLD STAFF

Published and printed
by arrangement with

St.Martin's Griffin

New York

DOWNTON ABBEY: RULES FOR HOUSEHOLD STAFF. Copyright ©
2014 by Justyn Barnes. Foreword Copyright © 2014 by Julian Fellowes. All
rights reserved. Printed in the United States of America. For information,
address St. Martin's Press, 175 Fifth Avenue, New York, N.Y. 10010.

Illustrations © David Hurtado, pp. 8–9, 16, 22, 25, 28, 36, 50, 52, 56, 61, 62,
63, 64, 76, 102; © Ruth Murray, pp. 18, 30, 31, 32, 35, 40, 47, 60, 75, 81, 83,
89, 90, 95, 96, 111.

A Carnival Films / Masterpiece Co-Production

Downton Abbey™ and Downton™ Carnival Film & Television Ltd

carnival

© 2005 Carnival Film & Television Ltd

Masterpiece is a trademark of the WGBH Educational Foundation

MASTERPIECE

www.stmartins.com

Library of Congress Cataloging-in-Publication Data

Downton Abbey, rules for household staff / introduction by Mr. Carson.
— First U.S. edition.
    p. cm.
Includes bibliographical references.
ISBN 978-1-250-06632-9 (paper over board)
ISBN 978-1-4668-7449-7 (e-book)
1. Downton Abbey (Television program) 2. Home economics—
Handbooks, manuals, etc. 3. Home economics—Great Britain—
Miscellanea. 4. Household employees—Handbooks, manuals, etc. 5.
Household employees—Great Britain—Fiction. 6. Country houses—Great
Britain—Fiction.
  TX331.D69 2014
  640'.46—dc23

2014034637

St. Martin's Griffin books may be purchased for educational, business, or
promotional use. For information on bulk purchases, please contact the
Macmillan Corporate and Premium Sales Department at 1-800-221-7945,
extension 5442, or write specialmarkets@macmillan.com.

First published in Great Britain by Headline Publishing Group,
an Hachette UK Company

First U.S. Edition: November 2014

10   9   8   7   6   5   4   3   2   1

CONTENTS

FOREWORD

Nothing can be more discommoding in life to an orderly person than to enter a house, whether as a guest or a member of staff, without a proper knowledge of how things are managed there. As we all know, to be wrongly dressed is to ruin one's enjoyment of a party, and to be unconscious of the rules that are observed by a household is to render oneself a clumsy outsider, open to the derision of others and the just accusation of amateurism.

To avoid this, I have thought fit to assemble this little book of suggestions that I hope the aspirant servant, either at Downton Abbey or elsewhere, may find informative and useful. I say 'aspirant' because I write only for those employees who aim for the highest standards, who wish to master their chosen career to the satisfaction of all they come in contact with. Such has been my own ambition.

To be a servant, in my view, is a noble calling. I do not suggest that every Hall Boy who starts out blacking boots can expect to be the Butler of a great house, although some must achieve it, nor will every girl be a Lady's Maid to a peeress or a Cook for Crowned heads or run the house of a political leader although, again, some will. But even those who do not reach these heights can feel proud that the goal of service is to smooth the paths of others, to free them from care and leave them calm and able to devote their talents and education to the general good. Like doctors and nurses, we heal and make well lives that can be fraught with worry and responsibility, we make entertaining a pleasure, motherhood a joy, by taking on the elements of those roles that can be tiring and stressful. The Cook, the Nursemaid, the Valet, the Footman, the Gardener, can all lay claim to being Improvers of Life, an honour in itself.

I have been called a hard task-master and I do not shirk the charge. My first job was as a Junior Hall Boy at Thrushcross Grange near Ripon, where I arrived in 1870 at the age of fourteen. I found myself under the command of a Mr Alfred Beet, the sternest Butler I have ever encountered, but also in retrospect one of the fairest, a man of the highest possible standards who took pride in every challenge. He was certainly as hard a task-master when it came to his own work as he was with his team, nor can I pretend my efforts always pleased him. Many's the clip round the ear I can still feel for an un-shone shoe or a mis-ironed newspaper, but his approval, when it came, was a prize in itself which kept me going the whole day long, and I have tried to make him my model in the years since then. Under his stern tutelage, I progressed from Hall Boy to Nursery Footman, and then to Fourth Footman in charge of old Mr Earnshaw's clocks, but at last it was time to leave and at nineteen I took a position as Second Footman to the Earl of Grantham at Downton, where I have remained for the rest of my working life. The end of my term at the Grange was an important step for me and I can still remember Mr Beet's speech when we parted. 'I am pleased to say that you understand the duty of service, Mr Carson. You know the good it can do, and you take pride in that knowledge. God bless you.' The memory of that moment, I freely confess it, can still bring a tear to my eye. His words have stayed with me throughout the years, providing both discipline and solace through good times and bad, and I can only recommend them to anyone who seeks to enter our ancient, and honourable, profession.

Charles Carson
Butler to the Earl of Grantham
Downton Abbey
August 1924

INTRODUCTION

These are clear instructions for Downton Abbey staff in order to carry out their tasks in the most expeditious and satisfactory fashion. Compiled as an exhaustive set of rules for the newest, most inexperienced members of staff, it is recommended that even the most seasoned servants reacquaint themselves with these accurate directions from time to time.

Read not merely the directions under your own job title because there are some duties which are common to different servants, and you may find the information contained in these other sections useful in completing your own tasks. Particularly so in the event that another staff member is taken ill or indisposed, and you are asked to assume their responsibilities. Furthermore, reviewing the entire contents of this book will greatly assist you to understand your place in upholding the high standards of this household.

Lord and Lady Grantham take great pride in their estate, and servants are expected to show that same pride when carrying out their work because they are part of the estate and its ambassadors among servants from other households. Above and below stairs, we all share the duty of keeping the house in good order, something we expect to be passed on to generations to come. It is only by everyone understanding their role and discharging their daily duties efficiently that this will be achieved.

THE HIERARCHY OF STAFF

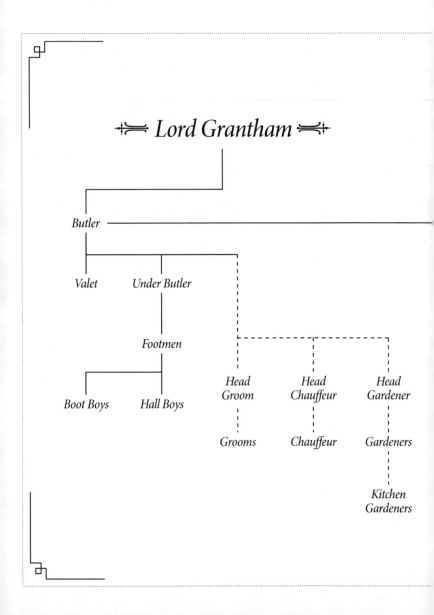

❧ Lady Grantham ❧

- Housekeeper
  - Ladies' Maids
  - Senior Housemaid
    - Housemaids
- Cook
  - Assistant Cook
    - Kitchen Maids
      - Scullery Maids

GENERAL NOTES AND INSTRUCTIONS FOR THE ATTENTION OF ALL HOUSEHOLD SERVANTS

SERVANTS' QUARTERS

We regard Downton Abbey as not just the home of the Crawley family, but also of the servants. It is a large house and estate where the servants live and work, and the Crawleys wish to be fair employers. The servants' quarters and rooms are maintained by the Housekeeper and the family will not choose to enter these areas unless there are exceptional circumstances. There are also cottages on the estate which may be granted for married couples to occupy in very exceptional circumstances but marriage, while in service, is not encouraged because it will thwart advancement.

THE BENEFITS OF EARLY RISING

Early rising is an essential requirement of service, allowing you the chance to discharge the heaviest duties while the family are still asleep. In order to attend your duties well, they should be carried out at correct times and in the proper order. Without proper order, you shall inevitably lead yourself to a state of haste and confusion.

One can accomplish more work in one hour before the family are up than in two afterwards. By rising early, you secure the earliest opportunity of doing the dirtiest part of your work without interruption. It is extremely necessary to dress for purpose of the most unclean jobs, and never do so in the livery in which you attend to ladies and gentlemen of the house.

PERSONAL CLEANLINESS

Cleanliness with respect to the body

Cleanliness is the principal duty for all persons, because an unclean, or grimy, person is never of full health. Thus let the body be frequently washed with pure water, especially in summer when perspiration can be of a particularly clammy and malodorous nature. It is particularly necessary in hot weather to attend regularly to the armpits and feet as they perspire more.

When bathing, the scrupulous use of cloths and soft brushes is of great advantage to open the skin pores. Attention should be paid to the ears so that hearing shall not be impaired by the build-up of wax.

Take particular care to ensure that the face, hands and finger nails are perfectly clean at all times when above stairs addressing family and guests. Carry a handkerchief to ensure the nasal passages are kept clean, and all due efforts should be taken to ensure any sneezing be done away from family, food, and in the outdoors if possible to avoid spreading infectious germs. Do not sniff: if you need to blow your nose discreetly, strive to do so and never admit to a head cold.

Toenails should be kept short. Without regular attention they are liable to grow into the flesh and become a considerable and painful obstacle to walking. Equally, fingernails are to be kept short for reasons of sightliness and good hygiene.

Management of the teeth, throat and mouth

Washing the teeth every morning and evening shall be an essential part of your daily routine. Never retire to bed without having first cleaned the teeth with salt, lest food collected about their interstices during the day corrupt them at night.

Not only are unclean teeth unsightly and causal of malodorous breath, common toothache due to the hollow state of teeth originates in a want of regular cleanliness. The build-up of tartar shall, over time, injure the foundation of the tooth and eat away at the gums until they shall no longer be able to hold the tooth.

Toothbrushes and toothpaste may be obtained from the Housekeeper.

The use of a small piece of whalebone or sage leaf is also recommended to clean the tongue. Sage leaves are also useful in polishing the teeth.

To clean the throat, gargle with fresh water and swallow a mouthful every morning upon rising and before retiring.

DRESS

Never walk through the front of house unless in uniform and for reasons of work. Equally, Lord and Lady Grantham, other family members and guests will always endeavour to give advance warning if they are going to be walking through staff areas. A member of the kitchen staff will never have reason to venture upstairs through the baize door unless invited to in exceptional circumstances. However, the Cook will take the menus to Lady Grantham when called.

RESPECT

The most important law of service is to respect our elders and betters: in particular Lord and Lady Grantham and the Crawley family. We do not discuss the business of the house with strangers.

Never speak ill of your master or mistress, and always defend their reputations from any malicious insinuations or aspersions. Upholding their reputation and that of the household will only improve your own reputation as a loyal servant.

Offer the same respect and attention to the children, relatives and friends of your master and mistress as you do to them. If you do not, you are effectively disrespecting them, too. Even a pet that is loved by the family or guests should be given the same respect by a servant, and in no way ill-treated. We, in turn, are respected by Lord Grantham by his generous employment and trust.

BELL BOARD

It is of the utmost importance for everyone to pay attention to the bell board by which the family and guests call to summon assistance. Each room in the house has a cord connected to a wire that rings a bell on the board – the bells are labelled so it can be immediately discerned in which room assistance

is needed and who should attend. For instance, Lady Grantham and other married women take breakfast in bed, and must be served promptly by their Lady's Maids upon sounding of their respective bells.

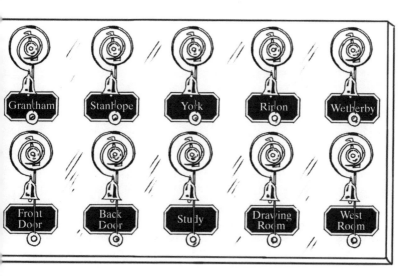

PERT ANSWERS

Humility is a useful qualification in all servants. Giving 'back answers' is a common fault among servants, and will not be tolerated by the Butler, Housekeeper or Cook. Muttering as you leave the room, slamming the door or marching heavily down the stairs is also unbecoming.

In such situations, it is always worth remembering the old proverb: 'Honey catches more flies than vinegar.' If your master or mistress scolds you (even without good cause), it is better to remain silent or speak mildly in response than give a pert, insolent reply. By remaining calm, when their anger has subsided, they will likely reflect kindly on your forbearance and make some atonement. In contrast, sharp replies may cause resentment in future. If you feel an injustice has been done and it needs to be addressed, bring it up later with the Butler, Housekeeper or Cook.

AVOIDANCE OF TALEBEARING

Be mindful not to tell tales. Those who cannot help to dispense tittle-tattle often tell more than they actually hear, and this may lead to unfortunate consequences. The best policy is to carry out your duties and not to interfere in the affairs of others. In this way, you will maintain a harmonious household and gain the admiration of your master, mistress, Butler, Housekeeper, Cook and fellow servants.

MODESTY

Live by the motto that: 'To say well is good, but to do well is better.' Always seek to cultivate modest and respectful behaviour that becomes your station, and refrain from being talkative or presumptuous. Boastfulness will only lower you in the estimation of others, whereas impressing by your actions and achievements will be talked of fondly by your master and acquaintances.

LISTEN & LEARN

Be open to learning from your master and mistress. They will have had many experiences and opportunities not open to a servant. Moreover, every person has their own way they like things to be done, and while it will make little difference to you, by doing it as they tell you, you will give satisfaction.

Furthermore, it pays for a young servant to follow the example of more experienced staff. There is a right way and a wrong way to do things – the former is easily acquired by attentive, observant young servants who do not fear to ask questions and these good habits will sustain you through your life and career. Bear in mind the more quickly and thoroughly you learn, the easier it will be for you to achieve a higher position in this household or to find a position, with good references, in another.

SERVANTS' MEALS

Servants' meals are prepared and served promptly by the kitchen staff, who will eat separately when instructed by the Cook. As a matter of courtesy, stand up from the dinner table when the Butler enters the room, and again when he leaves. If a member of the family should enter the room, servants should of course also rise.

FORETHOUGHT

With experience, you shall learn to anticipate the needs of the family, and this will both make you a better servant and your work more simple. Such forethought will allow you to, for example, make just one journey to carry items into the room when the less knowledgeable will take two trips.

However, until you know the family well, be wary not to presume to know their wishes so well that you do make mistakes. This fault through keenness is easily forgiven, but as you become accustomed to the family's ways, it is usually sufficient just to obey commands.

FRUGALITY

Remember that wastefulness is a sin. Frugality is necessary for your future welfare in life, so keep in mind that 'a penny saved is a penny got' both in regard to your own finances and the running of the household. Great waste often takes place with leftover food, the end of candles, bits of soap &c. thrown away. It may 'only' be a bit of dry bread thrown in the bin, but if you add up all the 'only's in a large household such as Downton over a year, it can amount to a great deal. Take the attitude that everything is of consequence and save for yourself and your employer.

SOBRIETY

All staff must be sober when on duty and due temperance with regard to alcohol is advised when in free time. Over time, a man's health will deteriorate due to drunkenness and it will cause failings in his character. It leads men to frequent public houses, spend their money unwisely and render them unfit for work.

One dram in the morning will destroy health more quickly than two in the evening, and excessive dram drinking, while cheering at the time, will be damaging in the end.

If a servant feels himself fatigued at any time by too much work, it is wise to remember the old proverb which says that: 'The smaller the drink, the cooler the head, and the cooler the blood'. At such times, a glass or two of good strong beer will refresh him more than a dram or two of spirits.

GOOD TEMPER

To earn the respect of the Crawley family and live in harmony with fellow servants here, one must maintain a good, even temper.

If you always endeavour to please, you shall rarely fail to do so and when you do make mistakes they will be more easily forgiven by your master or mistress, safe in the knowledge that your error arises not from disobedience or indolence. Masters and mistresses have too many concerns of their own to also deal with ill-tempered servants.

If you are at first deficient in carrying out the business for which you are employed, but willing to learn, you shall be instructed in what you are ignorant of without anger. Obstinacy and indolence, on the other hand, shall not meet with such kindness. There is no room for sulkiness or sullen behaviour in service. If you are fearful of offending, that very fearfulness indicates your respect for those you serve and a desire for their approval.

In short, a good temper is the most valuable of attributes and will ease its possessors through every challenge of service.

FELLOW SERVANTS

In a busy household it is easy to fall into quarrels with fellow servants. Take care not to let your anger rise over every trifling issue, and if someone is quarrelsome towards you, do your best to dampen their aggression. At such times, it should be at the forefront of your mind that no disturbance is caused to the family and the smooth running of the household.

If you have argued with one of your colleagues, do not attempt to take revenge on him or her by speaking ill of them to family members or do anything to spite or cast blame upon them. If discovered by the Butler, such behaviour will do you more harm than the person whose reputation you intended to injure. It is advised that when a problem arises, you instead seek the immediate counsel of the Butler or the Housekeeper, so that they may act to resolve the disagreement.

Also, be wary that not everyone may share your sense of humour, so be mindful not to offend others.

Female members of staff are reminded to be circumspect in their behaviour towards male servants. Behave with civility, but don't become overly familiar in a way that is unladylike and inappropriate.

VISITORS' SERVANTS

We often welcome guests with their own Valets and Maids to Downton Abbey. While we expect them to adhere to our way of attending tasks, it is to be expected that they may have practices peculiar to us. This is particularly so in regards to Americans, who can be more forward in their manner than is our custom. We should be understanding of their idiosyncrasies, while remaining steadfast in promoting and pursuing the high standards which have well served the household for many years. Be careful not to loosen your tongue about the Crawley family's life because your stories will quickly reach the ears of the visiting staff, master and mistress. Likewise, it is not a polite servant that seeks gossip from those who visit.

HONESTY

Honesty is so essential a qualification that a man or woman who does not possess it cannot be a good servant.

Be truthful in all your endeavours. If you make an error or are accused of a fault, do not make it worse by attempting to cover it up with a falsehood. If there is a breakage of an object, report it immediately because it will surely become known eventually and the carelessness of the breakage is compounded by the far greater fault of attempting to deceive your master or mistress.

To acknowledge your mistake and accept the blame is the quickest way to obtain forgiveness and earn the trust of others. Your master or mistress may often overlook your many small faults, for they are inevitable, so long as they know you to be honest.

CAREFULNESS

In the course of your work, you will be handling or in close proximity to many valuable things which may be damaged or destroyed due to lack of care. Want of care does more harm than want of knowledge, so the quality of care is highly desirable in all servants.

BUTLER

This entire book of rules has been compiled under the supervision of Mr Carson, Downton Abbey's esteemed Butler of longstanding. He has kindly agreed to explain the fundamental aspects of the Butler's job for the benefit of any servant who, in the unlikely event that Mr Carson is incapacitated, may be called upon to assume such duties.

As the most senior member of staff, the Butler of Downton Abbey is the ultimate conduit between the family and the serving staff below stairs, directly responsible to Lord Grantham. Absolute integrity and honesty are required in this position. While it may appear to others that practical duties of this role are few, it is his experience, eye for detail and timely direction of staff that will ensure that the highest possible standards are maintained throughout each day.

The Butler is in charge of hiring, disciplining and, if necessary, dismissing male servants. It is the Butler's responsibility to oversee the work of the Under Butler and Footmen, and ensure that the former trains the latter to become Valets – the visits of guests without servants offer opportunities for them to gain valuable experience.

The Butler looks after her Ladyship's jewels and the finest pieces of family silver (see page 19). He is also entrusted with managing the wine cellar, extending to the proper decanting and service of wines (see page 19).

In summary, the Butler must be constantly vigilant to ascertain and attend to the needs of the family.

DRESS

The Butler's uniform is provided by the family and fitted by a preferred tailor – either on the estate, in Downton village or in Ripon – for immaculate presentation.

CLEANING & STORAGE OF FINE SILVER

While many cleaning tasks shall be assigned to lower servants, the Butler is expected to clean and care for the most valuable items of silver.

Fine silver may often be stored for extended periods, so it is vital to polish it before putting it away. The silver cupboards and drawers are lined with paper, but the individual items should also be wrapped to protect them from dust. If wrapped well, silver will retain its shine and be immediately ready for use when unwrapped again.

Larger items of silver tableware should either be placed in a soft fabric bag if available or in non-acid tissue paper. If using tissue paper, place two or three sheets between plates, because one piece can easily slip and allow the silver surfaces to collide. Tuck the ends of the paper neatly underneath each item.

Wrap sets of knives, forks, spoons &c. separately in tissue paper so that they are easily identifiable. The parcels are then placed side by side in the silver drawer so that each piece of cutlery is on its side, rather than one bottom piece taking all the weight of the others.

INVENTORY OF FINE SILVER

In such a large household, it is important to keep a record of valuables in the house, and the Butler catalogues all items of fine silver. Each entry should have a brief description, a note of the year in which the item was made and the purchase price (if known). He shall also organise for the silver to be reappraised on a yearly basis for insurance purposes.

MANAGEMENT OF THE CELLAR

The word 'Butler' has its origins in the French word *bouteillier*, from the word *bouteille* (bottle), so it follows that there are few more important functions for a Butler than attending to the storage and service of every wine to ensure its quality. This extends to thorough cleaning of his decanters, inside and out, and the pride taken in the condition of the glasses in which he serves fine wines (see page 25).

Choice of wines

The Butler is not expected to choose the wines independently, but to advise his Lordship to deal only with wine merchants who are experts in their field and have his full confidence. However, it is the job of the Butler to check that the wines are not defective when received and, by following the tried and tested techniques outlined in this guide, keep them so that they are not injured, and served to best advantage.

Temperature

~ Gas burners or any other mode of heating should never be used in the cellar, as changes in temperature will cause the ruination of wine.

Even temperature – not varying by more than 2 or 3 degrees Fahrenheit – is vital for the development of wine as it is living matter containing a certain number of microbes. The wine undergoes a dormant fermentation which purifies it each spring and autumn. Maintaining an even temperature will allow this seasonal fermentation to occur naturally and advantageously to the development of the wine with age.

The same rules of even temperature apply to wines received in bottles as to those in casks.

~ Sparkling wines or madeiras do not undergo the same six-monthly action. The presence of carbonic acid gas in sparkling wines prevents fermentation, while madeiras are made in hot stores, which kill the microbes.

However, the same even temperature rules apply to their storage, as changes in temperature causes leakage through their corks.

~ No matter what measures are taken, as heat rises, the cellar will always be slightly warmer at the ceiling than on the floor. It is important therefore to take this into account when storing wines. For instance, the flavour and maturity of sherry improves with moderate warmth, so high placement is beneficial.

In contrast, champagnes and the even lighter hocks and moselles require very cool storage.

Thus the following placement is recommended:

> TOP: sherries, sauternes, madeiras and marsalas
> MIDDLE: clarets, ports, burgundies
> LOWER: sparkling wines, hocks, moselles

~ If unforeseen problems are encountered with heat regulation in the cellar, which would prevent storing the wines in such a manner, it is recommended that they are binned in sawdust, which does not conduct heat. However, packing in sawdust does increase the possibility of corks being attacked by insect life. To protect against this danger, and maximise the life of the cork, the Butler should dip every bottle in pliable wax or, even better, a resin solution (see page 21).

Bottling

*Bottling is not done at Downton Abbey anymore, and has not been done here,
in Mr Carson's memory, since the Benedictine monks occupied the buildings that form
the foundations to Lord Grantham's house. However, a summary of the
process is included here for interest:*

Only casks containing wine that has matured enough to be bottled should be accepted into a cellar. With red wine the test for judging the wine's readiness is that there is no purple tinge in the bead (bubbles) or froth. White wines which are hazy are not to be bottled. Then, of course, there should be nothing unpleasant or harsh to the palate.

Enough bottles and corks to bottle off an entire cask in one day are prepared – if this is not done the remaining wine will likely be unfit for bottling the next day.

Only the finest-quality corks available should be used, each about one and a half inches long – it is best not to use too long a cork as they are harder to draw and the less surface of cork in contact with the wine, the better. Buying cheaper corks is a false economy, as the wine is valuable, and a poor cork may spoil it.

Corks should be stored in a warm, perfectly dry place and checked to ensure that they are dry when brought out for use.

Bottling machines are now used by many bottling firms, but the old-fashioned 'boot and flogger', while more labour-intensive, is the only way to ensure wines are properly corked. Each bottle is placed in the leather case (boot) for safety, and the cork tapped in using the wooden flogger tool.

Once complete, the cork and rim of the bottle is brushed to remove all dust, and then dipped in wax or resin deep enough that the neck is well covered.

Filled bottles should be left standing up for two days before being binned in case they burst.

Notes on bottling clarets and burgundies

Clarets and burgundies require a little air to accelerate the maturing process without injuring the wine, so the cork is pierced with a sewing needle and half an inch left between the wine and the cork. (Wines bottled with the needle have no pressure of compressed air so they may be binned away at once.)

It is very difficult to assess the proper time to bottle a claret – a few months can make a huge difference. When fit for the bottle, it should be such that the wine can be enjoyed from the cask with a meal and without a harsh after-taste.

A needle is not used with ports, madeiras, sherries and marsalas, but a little more space – three-quarters of an inch to an inch, maximum – is left between wine and cork.

Binning

Careless binning causes breakages and the loss of good wine, so it must be carried out with military precision. The bins in the cellar have solid foundations so that the weight of every bottle may be evenly spread and supported. The bottles should be perfectly horizontal. Wedge in pieces of oaken laths between the last bottle and the wall to prevent any slippage when the top is filled with bottles.

Cellarage of bottled wines

When the Butler receives bottled wines rather than casks, he must adhere to the following checkpoints:

1. Examine each bottle for any leakage from the cork.

2. Bin away the wine in good condition.

3. Wines that are not perfectly bright and have deposits visible at the neck of the bottle should be stood up for a few days until those deposits have sunk to the bottom before being laid down in the bin.

4. Enter details in the Cellar Book:

   • thorough description of wine

   • purchase price

   • date of bottling

   • date of binning

   • quantity

   • use date/special comments

5. When a bottle is taken out, mark it off in the Cellar Book with the date when used so that stock levels can be easily monitored and checked. The balance will be carried forward to the next year's Cellar Book. Note should also be made of any spoiled wines (see page 24).

Dealing with decayed corks

With older wines, there is a great danger that the corks will be decayed or rotten. To clear a bottle of a rotten cork, you will need an intensely heated iron pair of circular tweezers.

Place the wine bottle on the cellar table. Very old wines will usually allow the standing up of the bottle because the deposit is so concentrated that it will not cloud the wine. If in any doubt, place the bottle in a decanting basket, which keeps it at an angle less likely to disturb the deposit.

Whether upright or angled, clasp the neck of the bottle just below the cork with the red-hot prongs of your tweezers and hold there for about half a minute.

Release and then pass a wet cloth over the neck. The neck will crack and come off cleanly allowing you to remove the cork with no chance of splinters falling into the wine.

Beware of 'scud'

Some white wines are prone to 'scud' disease, so called because it creates particles which scud about in the liquid when moved. It is caused by insufficient alcohol in the wine. Of all the diseases in white wines, this is the most likely to occur and most difficult to counter. Scud is infectious, so such wines must be disposed of without delay.

Decanting

Always decant 3-4 hours before serving. Careful decanting is required to present wines at their optimum and therefore precise instructions are necessary:

1. Place muslin over the decanter and light a candle nearby

2. Take the chosen bottle of wine out of the bin by the neck with a steady hand and lay it down on the table, making sure it cannot move.

3. Put the corkscrew into the cork, holding the bottle tightly with your other hand

4. Adjust to an angle where the wine no longer touches the cork inside the bottle and extract the cork without shaking the bottle in any way.

5. With one hand, raise the bottle above the level of the candle so you can see through the body of the bottle, making sure that the wine flowing into the decanter is 'candle bright' – appearing pure, uncloudy and bright. A clear wine tastes better.

6. Stop pouring as soon as a cloud or deposit approaches the neck of the bottle. The muslin is in place as a last resort to prevent natural deposits entering the decanter, but with careful pouring this shall not be needed.

Some general guidance regarding serving wine and other drinks

The Butler should have an instinct for what, when and how to serve wines. This instinct shall be honed by a thorough knowledge of every wine in the cellar, the guidance of his trusted wine merchants, his own taste and also by paying attention to the comments of family and guests at the table.

~ Every wine served should pass the 'candlebright test' outlined above.

~ Decanters and glasses should be sparkling clean, polished by cloth and then leather.

~ Wine found to be defective on decanting must not be served. This may be detected by the bouquet or lack of bouquet and, at worst, a corky or fungous smell. If it is not too bad, the wine may be put aside for use in cooking, but otherwise it should be discarded. Such wastage can be limited by following the good bottling techniques outlined above.

~ Oysters require the lightest possible still moselle hock or Chablis. A sweet or sparkling wine will overpower the flavour of the oysters and one glass is sufficient unless, of course, another is asked for.

~ After hot soup, the palate is alive and therefore it is important to serve the finest quality wine while the soup plates are being removed. A glass of sherry, madeira, Hungarian tokaji, or even a rich champagne would be appropriate.

~ In some houses, dry champagne is served throughout dinner, but such vulgar showboating merely demonstrates gastronomic ignorance. For instance, champagne after fish is a disaster (dry champagne should only be served with the roast). A fine claret served after pudding tastes tart and is a grave error.

The rule at Downton is simple: everything in its place. From the Butler's own knowledge and experience, and that of the wine merchant and the Cook, wines may be paired correctly. Here are some examples:

- white fish with a plain sauce – hock or Chablis

- heavier fish such as salmon – sauterne or a fine and fruity hock

- game – burgundy

- roast – a fine claret

- cheese – port, sherry or madeira

Serving vintage port

To truly enjoy an aged vintage bottle after dinner, it is best to build up to it by serving two younger, more fruity and powerful wines beforehand. This way the veteran port will be best appreciated.

ROYAL VISITS

While Lord Grantham is the Lord Lieutenant of Yorkshire, Downton Abbey must always be prepared to host Their Majesties The King and Queen or other members of the Royal Family if their duties call them to the county. His Lordship will be informed by the Private Secretary of the relevant Royalty's Household and her Ladyship will discuss the plan with Lord Grantham before issuing the relevant invitation as a formality. At this point his Lordship will inform the Butler, and her Ladyship will inform the Housekeeper and instruct the Cook to prepare menus for consideration.

All staff will be expected to maintain the strictest confidence.

In due course the police will contact Mr Carson to discuss the necessary security arrangements.

It should be assumed that in the case of Their Majesties visiting, all the Abbey's rooms will be required for the accompanying Suite. Lord Grantham will be informed of any particular needs or requirements and Lady Grantham may be informed by The Queen's Lady-in-Waiting of any required trifles.

Whilst the staff are always to be trusted as part of their employment, they are to be informed only when necessary and then reminded to be totally confidential. The house may need to be flexible in its strict schedule, which could put a strain on the domestic staff. Also the larger number of Royal staff will need to be appropriately housed, fed and supported during the sojourn. The household, in its temporary disorder and strain, must show neither to the visitors and reflect only what a great honour it is for the Abbey.

HOUSEKEEPER

This is a role of the greatest importance, requiring excellent qualities to facilitate the smooth running and upkeep of the household. The Housekeeper shall be responsible for overseeing the maintenance of all the domestic staff, seeing to their welfare while ensuring that the duties of the female staff are discharged properly on a daily basis. She will instil the importance of punctuality, method and attention to detail in all matters, inspiring them through her own example and being vigilant to any slackening of standards.

The Butler is responsible for the male servants and is ultimately the arbiter of discipline for all, so the Housekeeper will oversee the work of female servants (excepting elements of the work carried out by the Lady's Maid and the Cook).

THE DAILY ROUNDS

Lady Grantham will direct her wishes to the Housekeeper or Butler, and a card listing the planned activities for Lord and Lady Grantham, family members and guests will be drawn up in consequence.

The Housekeeper shall supervise the Head Housemaid and Housemaids in their daily rounds, to include:

~ Fire-laying, sweeping and dusting.

~ Making the written rota for cleaning of principal rooms and seeing that it is followed.

~ Making ready all public rooms before breakfast.

~ Making beds after breakfast – sheets are changed once per week (twice for mistress).

~ Upkeep of the servants' quarters.

SPRING CLEANING

In winter, the necessity to light and attend to fires means that the staff are particularly busy and unable to do much more than carry out their everyday tasks. It is best therefore to plan for bigger, irregular jobs to be done in springtime when the weather is temperate and they have more spare time. Spring offers the chance for papering rooms, painting walls, taking up carpets, checking every nook and cranny, disposing of unwanted articles &c.

Larger jobs and more thorough cleaning may also be attended to at other times of the year when many members of the family are away.

>━┤◆>━○━<◆┤━<

THE STORE ROOM

The Housekeeper shall hold the key to the store room and open it as required for the domestic staff.

LINEN

Many linen items are required to be ordered, prepared and maintained to effect the smooth running of the household. For example:

~ bed linen.

~ working linen: for instance, tea towels for drying dishes, oven cloths, round towels for drying hands, fine linen cloths for straining soups and scraps.

~ for the Housemaid: cloths and towels.

~ for the Butler and Footmen: linen towels and thin, pure linen squares for drying the silver.

It is the Housekeeper's responsibility to ensure that there is plentiful supply. Therefore, regular time should be put aside to examine the linen, arrange for mending if needed or order new items as replacements.

BOOK-KEEPING

It is a condition of employment that the Housekeeper shall have the necessary qualifications to understand accounts and, as such, she shall keep accurate records of sums paid for any expenses associated with the running of the house.

Often services are carried out by tradesmen or goods are delivered to the household for which payment is made later. These jobs/items must be logged at the time and bills that are later supplied must be checked against the agreed price and any discrepancies taken up with the supplier.

Each month, these accounts must be checked to ensure they are correct and within agreed budgets. By careful monitoring of accounts in all areas, it is expected that the Housekeeper shall eliminate any wasteful expenditure. For instance, it is advised that soap powder and other cleaning essentials are bought in bulk quantities from London on a quarterly basis.

All bills should be taken to the master or mistress who shall write out cheques.

It is understood that the Housekeeper may be entitled to a 'tip' or 'commission' from suppliers she favours with regular custom.

SPECIFIC NOTES PERTAINING TO
HOUSE PARTIES

The arrival of guests is a chance to show Downton Abbey at its best, and the great pride that our family and servants take in maintaining the highest standards. Our aim is that every guest leaves with the distinct impression of a well-run household. To achieve this we must carry out detailed planning in advance, and it is worth listing some of the specifics here for reference:

~ The Countess will decide upon which bedrooms will be used and inform the Housekeeper.

~ Her Ladyship shall also consult with the Cook on menus for the duration of the guests' stays. Once agreed, menus shall be written in French. Her Ladyship will also decide on the placement of guests around the table in advance.

~ The Housekeeper shall ensure that the chosen guest bedrooms are made up on the day of arrival and arrange freshly-cut flowers in each room.

~ The chauffeur will arrive at the station in good time to greet guests arriving by train.

~ The Butler shall assemble the Footmen (unless detained on work deemed too important to delay) alongside him and the family at the front door ready to greet esteemed guests.

~ Guests who arrive without a Valet or Lady's Maid shall be assigned a Footman (by the Butler) or Housemaid (by the Housekeeper).

~ Guests' luggage shall be unpacked in the luggage room. At this point, it is imperative that Maids compare dresses planned to be worn, lest anything too similar be worn at the same time.

~ Special requirements of the guests – such as delivery of newspapers or breakfast to their room – will be listed in the daily log book, and such extra tasks assigned to staff as appropriate.

~ When morning tea trays are delivered to guest rooms, open the curtains quietly but wake the guests firmly and remind them at what time breakfast is served.

~ When large numbers of guests are at the dining table, in addition to the Footmen, the Valet may be asked to assist with service. The Butler may also help if necessary, but Maids will not serve the table – the only exception to this rule would be in wartime.

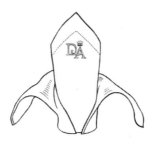

VALET

PARTICULAR QUALITIES

Discretion is of particular importance, as a Valet works closely with his master and may be party to private comments and discussions that are not for the staff to hear or public knowledge. He must therefore be very mindful of what he says and how he behaves. Even though the Valet will obviously form friendships with other members of staff, it is prudent that he maintain a little distance in conversation to remain faithful to his master.

The same rule applies when travelling. For instance, when aboard ship and the Valet is spending a lot of time with the crew, it is important that he build good relations (see 'Travel' notes on page 50), without being indiscreet. Passengers may also speak to him in the hope of an introduction to his employer. Caution should always be the watchword in such circumstances.

DRESS

Valets will always dress with the utmost smartness – single-pleat trousers and three- or four-button jacket is advised, and a shirt with an Albany or double round collar. On occasion the Valet may be offered clothes his master no longer needs for his own use.

SPECIAL ADVICE FOR THE VALET SERVICE OF THE EARL OF GRANTHAM

Lord Grantham's personal Valet shall be ready for all eventualities. Your principal duties in the service of his Lordship may be summarised as follows:

~ Making sure Lord Grantham is properly turned out at all times.

~ Travelling with him wherever he goes. Being responsible for packing the correct attire without being asked.

~ Carrying out any spot-cleaning or mending.

~ Being on hand at all times to assist his lordship – for example, have his hat, coat, gloves, boots and cane ready if he decides to go for a walk.

Daily routine

1. Take up a calling tray with tea upon it.

2. Brush and lay out his Lordship's clothes for the day.

3. Attend to the dressing room and bedroom – make sure the fires are lit, rooms are dusted and cleaned by the Housemaids and collect any clothes requiring cleaning and mending.

4. Help his Lordship with five to seven changes of clothing per day.

• Cedar-lined cupboards are available in the attic for storage of clothes not often worn. These are particularly useful for seasonal rotation of summer and winter clothes.

• Lord Grantham tends to wear certain sets of studs and links for certain occasions – for an ordinary dinner, a ball, a visit to London &c. – but for the absence of doubt, it is best practice to lay out all before him to make a choice.

• His Lordship has a collection of snuff boxes which are most precious to him, so these must be handled with the utmost care.

GENTLEMAN'S DRESSING ROOMS

When entering in the morning, before the gentleman gets up (in winter) see that the Housemaid has lit the fire, and cleaned out and dusted the rooms.

Put out all the washing things/items necessary to his ablutions so they are at hand. Fill the water bottle with spring water and the bath with hot water. Air your master's dressing gown and slippers by the fire. See that the tooth, hair and nail brushes are clean and lay them out neatly. Set the razor with a piece of cloth to wipe the razor on. Should he shave with boiling water, be sure to have it at his disposal.

The coat, trousers and other things intended to be worn must be laid out neatly. Also place a shoehorn next to his chosen shoes for the day.

Once the gentleman is dressed and has left the room, take the earliest opportunity to stir the fire and clean and return everything to its proper place ready for use again. Brush and press every garment that has been taken off and put them away. Check the brushes and combs are clean – if they require washing, use soap and hot water, wipe them as dry as possible and then place at a safe distance from the fire, bristles-downwards. When completely dry, put them in their proper places. Strop the razor. Place towels that are not dirty on the towel-horse to dry and change those that are for clean ones.

Stropping a razor

Gentlemen who shave themselves often strop their own razors immediately after use whilst still warm. If left to you, dip the razor in warm water, and wipe dry with a rag. Then lay it flat on the strop and, holding it lightly, draw it diagonally from heel to the point the whole length of the strop, turn over the blade and stroke back up the strop. A dozen strokes on each side of the blade will keep the razor in good condition for a considerable time.

To prepare razor strops

Glue pieces of soft leather to either side of a piece of wood. When the glue has set, rub one side over with a little sweet oil (leave the other side plain leather). Then spread thinly over the oiled leather with some very fine emery powder or oxide of iron and roll over the surface with a small bottle to flatten. Razors may be kept with a fine edge using this strop and the directions given above.

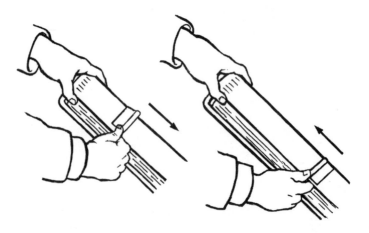

A WASH TO PREVENT A GENTLEMAN'S HAIR
FALLING OUT

If your master should express concern about the prospect of impending baldness (and *only* if, for it is a sensitive subject), you may suggest the following preventative wash.

To make, take a quarter of an ounce of unprepared tobacco leaves, two ounces of rosemary, two ounces of box leaves and boil together in a quart of water in an earthenware 'pipkin' pot with a lid, for twenty minutes.

Strain and use this wash cold, by applying to the hair roots with a hairbrush occasionally during the summer months.

CLEANING BOOTS & SHOES

It is to be recommended that cleaning of boots and shoes is attended to early in the day, for it is a dirty job and they may be required at any time with no advance notice.

To complete this task, the following items are indispensable:

Old newspaper	A small painter's brush
A wooden knife	Blacking
Good brushes – for cleaning, blacking and polishing	Soft cloth

1. If drying is required before cleaning, lay the shoes or boots down at a proper distance from the fire, or the leather will harden.

2. Pack them with old newspaper.

3. Should you have topped boots to clean, cover the tops with a little paper or parchment, so that you may have the freedom to clean to the top edge without dirtying them.

4. Remove excess dirt from each shoe or boot, using a wooden knife. Steel knives should be avoided – unless they are exceptionally blunt – for they are liable to cut the leather.

5. Use a hard brush to remove all dust or the leather will never brighten.

6. Stir up the blacking thoroughly with the painter's brush.

7. Put a little blacking on the blacking brush and apply all over the leather uppers.

8. While the blacking is still damp, apply the polishing brush immediately to bring up a rich jet black.

9. Buff vigorously with the soft cloth to shine.

To clean boot tops – white

1oz oxalic acid   1 pt soft water

Dissolve the oxalic acid in the water and keep in a firmly corked bottle. Be sure to label the bottle 'Poison' for it is highly toxic.

For cleaning, apply the mixture with a soft sponge. Then rub the tops with a little fine bath brick dust, and sponge the tops afterward with a little cold water.

To clean boot tops – brown

1pt skimmed milk   1oz gum Arabic
½oz spirits   juice of 2 lemons
½oz spirits of lavender

Mix well together and keep the liquid in a bottle well corked. Rub the tops with the mixture using a sponge, but use no brick dust. When the tops are dry, polish with a flannel or brush.

Waterproofing

1 pt drying oil   2oz turpentine
2oz yellow wax   ½oz Burgundy pitch

Mix the ingredients carefully over a slow fire. Apply the mixture while hot over the boots or shoes with a sponge. Wait until they are dry and then lay it over again and again until quite saturated. Then let them be put away and not worn until completely dry, whereupon the leather will be found to be not only impenetrable to damp for longlasting, but soft and pliable for greater comfort.

To stop boots and shoes creaking

Soak the soles in salted water and then leave them for at least ten hours in linseed oil.

COATS – BRUSHING

Great care should be taken in brushing your master's clothes and your own so as not to injure them. The brushing movement should be a firm sweeping motion. Never 'scrub' back and forth. Start with a smooth brushstroke against the nap of the cloth to disturb any trapped dust and dirt. Shorter, faster strokes may be applied to remove more stubborn marks, but always finish by brushing with the lie of the cloth for a smooth, unruffled finish.

Required for this task:

A wooden horse
A small hand whip or cane
A board or wooden table at
least as long as the item to be
brushed

2 natural bristle brushes –
one hard bristle, one soft

The hard bristle brush may only be used on heavy coats. Fine cloth coats must never be brushed with too stiff a bristle, as this will make them look bare in short time. Use a new brush on old cloth to wear down the bristles a little.

If a small hand whip is not available, be careful in choosing the cane, that it is not too large or has too uneven knots. When beating the lint and dust out of a coat, do not hit too hard as it is easy to strike holes into a coat. Always be careful not to hit the buttons with a cane, for it will scratch or even break them, so a small hand whip is preferable.

1. If a coat is wet, wait until dry before brushing.

2. Rub out any spots of dirt between your hands but take care not to rumple the cloth unduly in so doing.

3. If required, beat out the lint and dust as previously directed.

4. Lay out the coat on the board or table gently pressing the collar with the left hand and holding the brush in the right. Brush with quick and soft motions, as this will remove the dust and lint effectively and with minimal wear.

5. Brush the back of the collar first, between the two shoulders, then the sleeves, observing to brush the same way as the nap of the cloth which is towards the skirts of the coat. Then attend to the front of the coat in the same way.

6. When both sides are properly brushed, brush the inside, and, last of all, the collar.

7. Hang the coat in its proper place, and at full length if the wardrobe height allows.

COATS – REMOVING GREASE

Grease must be removed from coats at the earliest opportunity lest it shows. Place brown paper on the part where the grease is and apply the end of a hot iron upon it. If the grease comes through the paper, put on another piece and iron until grease no longer comes through. Finally, wrap a little piece of flannel around your finger and dip in some spirits of wine and rub the area so that all traces of grease are removed.

Note that if the iron is too hot, it can discolour a garment, so be sure to test it beforehand by ironing the brown paper on the flannel – if the brown paper scorches, it must be allowed to cool first.

DRY CLEANING GLOVES

Lay the gloves on a clean board and, using a stiff brush, rub them over on each side with a finely powdered mixture of dried Fuller's earth and alum. Then sweep off the powder, sprinkle them with dry bran and whiting and dust them thoroughly.

This process should be enough to make gloves quite clean, but, if they are much soiled, first take out any grease with warm toasted bread, then apply the former mixture with a woollen cloth. This dry method is a safer option than wetting the gloves which frequently shrinks and spoils them.

TO FRESHEN UP CLOTHES

While you should always allow clothes to dry before brushing, sometimes a slightly damp brush can freshen up clothes after first applying the dry brush.

Simply add half a capful of ammonia to a pint of water (note: do not be tempted to add any more ammonia than this as it will turn a black suit green!). Submerge the bristles of the brush in the liquid and then flick away excess liquid until the bristles are just damp. Then brush normally.

It is also important to air clothes regularly in the airing cupboard. This is essential after ironing which will leave slight dampness in the material that could cause a chill if worn next to the skin.

Also, after a long journey or a visit to his club in London, your master's clothes may take on the strong smell of stale tobacco. On a warm day, hanging any affected garment outside in the fresh air is the best remedy.

THE PROPER CARE OF HATS

Without diligent care, a hat will soon look lacklustre. A soft camel-hair brush will keep the fur smooth without scratching it off.

There is a stick for each hat which must be used to keep it in its proper shape when it has got wet. Put the stick in as soon as it is taken off, and only when dry transfer it to a hat box. Air and dust will turn hats brown, so storage in the hat box is essential.

If the hat has got very wet, handle lightly or you may crack or break the felt.

Wipe it as dry as you can with a silk handkerchief, then brush it with a soft brush in the same direction as the fur lay when dry. Do not apply a hard bristle brush to a wet hat.

When it is nearly dry, you may use a harder bristle if fur still sticks so close that you cannot get it loose. Applying a sponge dipped in beer or vinegar will help to loosen, and then brush it with a hard brush until dry.

PARTICULAR NOTES PERTAINING TO THE CARE OF TOP HATS

Top hats may be covered in felt or with delicate silk plush material which you must treat especially carefully.

In either case, clean off dust very gently using a brush with the softest bristles, smoothing the nap lightly in an anti-clockwise direction.

To finish a silk plush hat, take a velvet pad and 'polish' it with the nap to bring up a bright sheen.

Ensure that any top hat is correctly stored, hanging it by the brim on the ledge of the box, thus taking the weight off it.

MAINTENANCE OF A POCKET WATCH

If your master's pocket watch is losing time, the fumes of paraffin will help to ease its workings.

Simply place a thimbleful of paraffin next to the watch and place under a glass bowl. Leave it there for a day to allow the fumes to be absorbed. When removed, the watch should be up to speed again.

STORAGE OF CLOTHES

Always put away discarded clothes in the proper place in the wardrobe as soon as possible – they must never be left lying around. Be aware that your master may remove an item from the wardrobe and put it back carelessly, so also check the clothes wardrobes and drawers at least once a day to make sure everything is neat and as it should be.

Suits

A three-piece suit is kept together on one double-barred wooden hanger.

~ Place the trousers over the centre of lower bar, folded over the bar about six inches above the knee.

~ Then hang the waistcoat. Make sure it is hanging straight by lining up the centre of the collar with the hanger's crook. Button up one button so it is easily ready for wear.

~ Put the jacket over the top, taking care not to upset the shoulders of the waistcoat beneath and, again, make sure it is centred on the hanger.

~ Pat down gently to make sure there are no wrinkles.

~ Pierce a large piece of tissue paper with the crook of the hanger so that it protects the shoulders and lapels from dust.

Coats

Use a single-barred hanger, but apply the same method and checks as for a suit jacket.

REMOVING BLOOD STAINS
FROM CLOTHING

Should your master be unfortunate enough to sustain an injury, perhaps when playing sport or hunting, your first concern of course will be for his welfare, but his garments must also be attended to. Bleaching may be the only option for older blood stains, but if the blood is freshly spilled, soak the garment in lukewarm, slightly salted water before scrubbing with washing soap.

DISPOSAL OF CLOTHING

If your master hands you some clothing to be thrown away as he no longer has any use for it, you may dispose of it. Although unspoken, it is also acceptable for you to keep such items to wear yourself if you wish. However, a very dim view will be taken of anyone taking items unbidden.

TRAVEL

In preparation for a trip, care should be taken to ascertain the probable time of absence, so that a sufficient change of clothes and linen (if necessary) may be provided.

Make a memorandum of all things that you are taking with you, not only of the items, but the numbers of parcels or boxes. Then each time a stop is made, check the list so that you quickly discover any loss and can replace it or report to your master.

When going on extended trips with his Lordship and the family, there will be many pieces of luggage to transport. If travelling abroad by boat, it may be expedient to travel to the dock ahead of the family with the luggage to make sure that it is all assigned to the correct cabins.

On rail journeys, see that all boxes and parcels are safely put into the luggage van, and accord the same vigilance when changing trains and at the final destination in order to secure the luggage.

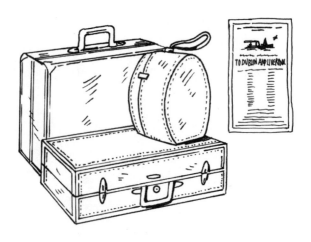

When arrived at hotels or visiting places, immediately ascertain your master's apartments, carry his belongings into the dressing room and lay them out for him.

It is your responsibility to ensure his Lordship has every comfort. To this end, it is necessary not only to speak to the manager, but also politely ask other members of staff for specific services. His Lordship may want his bed and other furniture in his room moved, in which case it is best to talk directly to the chambermaid. It may be the case he has special food requirements which are not part of the regular menu, so a visit to the kitchen will be the best way to fulfil his wishes.

It is also important when travelling to make sure your master's bed is not damp. To do so, use the following method:

To detect dampness in beds

Once the bed has been well warmed, remove the warming pan and place a glass tumbler inverted between the sheets. After a few minutes, examine the glass. If found dry, the bed is safe for sleeping in. If drops of wet adhere to the inside of the glass, it is a sure sign of a damp bed. In most parts of England, the application of a warming pan will cause a slight steam inside the glass, but not wet drops. If you find the bed damp, airing the sheets may solve the problem. If not, ask the hotel's management to provide a change of mattress or, if necessary, an alternative room.

LADY'S MAID

The Lady's Maid is on call for her mistress from the moment of waking until she retires to bed. The principal responsibility of this role is to make sure every detail of her mistress's clothing is well presented at all times – indeed, only the Lady's Maid is permitted to touch her mistress's dressing tables – and that her hair is immaculately styled.

Mending skills, tidiness and the ability to pack clothes correctly and speedily are essential. Being of good temper and reliability are vital qualities. A mistress will likely confide in her Maid, a privilege which requires absolute discretion.

A Lady's Maid shall be expected to dress in a smart and modest manner at all times.

MAIN DUTIES

~ Laying out clothes throughout the day for the lady to change into as requested. She may require up to seven changes of clothes.

~ Picking up and attending to discarded items; collecting clothes from the night before to be washed or pressed. Any day clothes not to be washed or pressed shall be covered so as not to be seen by a gentleman.

~ Assisting with dressing and hair-styling.

~ Cleaning and safely storing the lady's jewellery (note: Lady Grantham's finest jewellery is kept in the care of the Butler).

~ You will need to be proficient in fine-washing, fine-mending and fine-ironing so as to attend to your mistress's finest clothes, petticoats and underclothes. Selected items may be sent to specialist cleaners as required.

~ Delivering messages.

~ Shopping for the lady or accompanying her on shopping trips.

~ Arranging entertainments for the lady as requested – for instance, sewing or painting, trips to the village, visiting local friends.

~ Helping your mistress to get ready for bed at night and checking she has everything she needs before retiring.

~ Packing for a journey or overnight trip – no specific instructions may be given, in which case you will be entrusted to choose suitable items. Given time and experience, a good Lady's Maid will know what is required to cater for whatever engagements are planned and possible.

~ Accompanying your mistress on trips; ensuring that all trunks and hat boxes are safely stowed on the train or ship. It is of great benefit in this respect to tip a guard or porter well to assist. On train journeys, it is important to find a first-class compartment for your mistress, with a third-class seat for yourself as near as possible. This is understood by most with whom you book the journey.

SPECIAL NOTES ON CARE
OF CLOTHING & SHOES

Silks

White silks must be washed alone in lukewarm, soapy water – silks must never be boiled. Do not rub soap directly onto the silk, but instead move the article around and squeeze the fabric gently.

For stubborn stains, it may be necessary to dissolve salt in the water, and repeat the process.

Do not wring out the silk, but firmly press the material flat between the hands and dry in the shade.

With coloured silks, each colour must be washed separately, but using the same method as above. Adding salt to the water will help to clean browns and reds, whereas the addition of a little vinegar instead will aid the cleaning of blues, purples and greens.

To iron silks, do so while they are still damp with a moderately warm iron and cotton cloth placed over the silk to protect it. When the silk is almost dry, you may remove the covering and iron the silk directly.

Silk dresses are too delicate ever to be brushed. Instead use a piece of merino wool of a similar colour.

Fine lace

To clean the finest, most expensive, lace, sprinkle powdered magnesia on the material, and fold up, making sure there is magnesia on every part. Leave the lace item unmoved for a few days until the magnesia has absorbed the dirt.

To clean lace collars, rub the edge of the collar with linen cloth, then wash the edges with fine toilet soap. Spread the collar on an ironing board, pin carefully and dab with a sponge that has been dipped in water in which some gum-dragon and fig-blue has been dissolved.

Furs

For dark furs, rub the fur with bran moistened in hot water and then dry with a flannel. Shake out to remove all traces of the bran.

With white furs, dry Fuller's earth so it crumbles into a powder and sprinkle over the fur. Work the powder into the fur with a clean linen cloth and then leave. After an hour or more, take the fur outside and beat it till all the powder is removed. Apply a soft brush to the fur to finish.

Removing grease spots from clothes

Take dry Fuller's earth then moisten it well with lemon juice. Add a small quantity of pure pulverised pearl-ash and work the whole thing into a thick paste. Roll into balls and dry in the heat of the sun to make ready for use.

Moisten the grease spots on the affected cloth and apply the ball, then hang the clothes in the sun to dry.

Or sprinkle with powder and leave for 24 hours.

Polish for ladies' boots

As an alternative to blacking them, mix sweet oil, vinegar and treacle with 1oz of lamp black. Apply the mixture to the boots and place them in a cool place to dry.

Satin boots and shoes

Dust with a soft brush or wipe with a cloth.

Ironing

~ Make sure the iron, ironing board and ironing blanket are clean.

~ Beware of the varying temperature of the iron as the thermostat cannot always be relied on. If the iron is too hot, the material will burn; too cold, and you may cause a brown iron mould mark.

~ It is prudent to place a linen cloth on top of all clothes to be ironed to protect the cloth from undue wear. When ironing wool, tweed and corduroy, a wrung out but still slightly damp cloth should be used.

~ Iron lighter fabrics first, allowing the temperature of the iron to rise ready for the heavier ones.

~ While pressing clothes makes them appear well, ironing too regularly with the intense heat of the iron increases wear, so be wary of doing so too often.

To preserve clothes from moths

There are a variety of recommended ways to prevent a damaging invasion of moths. For example, placing the following in the drawers and on the shelves where clothes are kept:

~ cedar shavings

~ a tallow candle wrapped in paper

~ cuttings of Russian leather

~ pieces of camphor

~ lavender flowers, rose leaves and perfumes of all kinds

In addition to these measures, it is advisable to occasionally hang rarely-worn clothes out in the sun on a fine day to freshen them. Take the opportunity to clean the drawers, and brush the clothes before returning them to their places again.

HAIRDRESSING

Hairdressing is a most important skill for a Lady's Maid. You will have been trained in this, but as fashions so often change it is important that you read current magazines in your spare time to be aware of the latest styles. If you need to learn new techniques, ask your mistress and she may be willing to bear the expense of the lessons required. You must brush out your mistress's hair every night before bed and every morning before setting the hair.

How to properly clean a hairbrush

First, comb out any hair that is caught in the bristles. Then add a lump of soda the size of golf ball to a quart of hot water and let it dissolve. Do not use soapy water as this will make the bristles soften.

Dip the bristles in and out of the water – keeping the handle and back of the brush clear. When the bristles appear clean, rinse the brushes in cold water. Dry the handle and back with a cloth immediately but leave the bristles to dry naturally, by propping the brush up a safe distance from the fire or outside in sunshine.

Curling tongs

When assisting a lady with curling tongs, the utmost patience and care must be taken. Marcel Wave curling tongs may become too hot and injure the hair, but equally if used too cool, the curls will not set. If in doubt, it is better to err towards cooler, lest the lady's hair becomes damaged.

How to make pomatum for dry hair

After washing, hair may become dry and rubbing in a little pomatum with the palm of the hand will restore its gloss. To make it, you will need:

8oz olive oil	Drops of essential oil
1oz spermaceti	Drops of essence of lemon

Mix all these ingredients well and store the liquid in a jar ready for use.

A lotion to encourage the healthy growth of hair

Mix equal quantities of olive oil and spirit of rosemary with a few drops of oil of nutmeg. Rub this lotion into the roots of the hair each night.

JEWELLERY

When not in use, items of jewellery should immediately be placed back in their cases. But first check if they require cleaning, as exposure to the elements can, over time, cause them to lose their lustre. If so, any article of gold, silver or precious stones may be dipped in a soapy lye prepared from fine toilet soap. Dry off afterwards with a badger-hair brush and buff with chamois leather. At the end of the day, the jewellery should be placed in the strong room and signed in to the Inventory Book by the Butler, or the Butler of any house you are visiting.

PARTICULAR ADVICE FOR FEMALE SERVANTS
ON POSTURE & CARRIAGE

Above stairs, Maids and all staff are expected to carry themselves correctly at all times. To survey your posture, stand in front of a full-length mirror and check the following:

Feet

Your toes should point straight ahead, never toe out. The insides of your feet should be parallel whether standing or walking for grace and control and to ensure no unsightly waddling.

When standing still, your weight should fall neither through the heels nor balls of your feet – either of which would upset your balance – but directly through the centre of your ankle bones.

If your weight is correctly distributed over your arches and ankle bones, you will be able to lift either your toes or heels slightly off the floor without losing balance.

Knees

It is a habit that many carry their knees too stiffly, forcing the stomach to pop out and tension to spread through the body. Keep your knees soft and slightly flexed, for easy balance of your upper body on your legs. Flexed does not, of course, mean bent – that wouldn't do.

Hips

Hips should be at all times, walking or standing, folded down and under you in the same forward position you would assume to squeeze through a narrow space.

Chest

Assume a neutral position, neither thrust forward like a strutting peacock nor caved in like a broken reed.

Shoulders

Drop your shoulders down, not pulling forward or backward on your neck muscles. Avoid the temptation to throw them back (and consequently thrust out your chest) as this will cause severe muscle strain through your neck and back over time.

Head

The head should be poised aloft, perfectly centred over the neck, neither hanging forward as if it belonged to an exhausted donkey nor pulled back like an eager hound on a leash. Correctly positioned, you should be able to balance a cup of tea and saucer on it without fear of spillage.

If you are standing correctly, you will be lined up so that a straight line could be drawn from your ear lobe down through the outermost tip of your shoulder girdle, the outermost tip of your hip girdle to the outside bump of your ankle bone.

The ideal posture forms a straight line from ear to ankle.

Bending down correctly

When picking up something from the floor, avoid flopping over from the waistline, with legs straight and curving the back excessively to reach down.

Place one foot a short step in front of the other, and, keeping the head and back upright, bend the knees and thigh joints until you are down in reach of the object. Come back up the same way, pushing up with the rear foot.

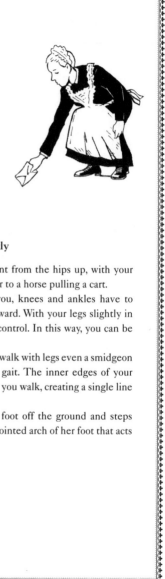

Walking correctly

Maintaining the same upper body alignment from the hips up, with your legs walking slightly ahead of your torso, similar to a horse pulling a cart.

If your legs are ramrod straight beneath you, knees and ankles have to tighten in order to keep you from pitching forward. With your legs slightly in front of you, you can walk smoothly and with control. In this way, you can be both quick and discreet in everything you do.

Female staff must take particular care not to walk with legs even a smidgeon too far apart, which begets a most unladylike gait. The inner edges of your knees should just graze each other in passing as you walk, creating a single line of footsteps behind you.

The quiet, graceful walker lifts her entire foot off the ground and steps down on it again, letting the weight fall on the jointed arch of her foot that acts as a natural air cushion.

COOK

The position of Cook is of great importance as she heads up the Kitchen Department, not only for the pleasure and sustenance her food may bring the family and guests, but also their good health.

Menus will be prepared in accordance with the produce and supplies available and offered up for the agreement of Lady Grantham. Then the necessary supplies ordered through the Housekeeper. For a large lunch or dinner party, the mistress and the Cook will discuss the menu at least a day before so that things that are possible to prepare in advance can be.

The Cook will send for the necessary fresh vegetables and herbs from the garden early in the day so that they may be delivered by the gardeners in time to be properly cleaned. She will also take care in maintaining sufficient stock of spices and condiments – discovering oneself short of a crucial ingredient at a late stage can cause avoidable delay.

Each course of every meal shall be served in timely fashion and at its best. This requires rigorous planning, methodical work and vigilant supervision of the kitchen staff's work. Some dishes may be cooked in advance and left to stand on the hot plate without injury to the food, but others more delicate require fine timing. Hot dishes and sauces intended to be hot are expected to be served hot! Here, the Cook relies on the Under Butler for the efficiency of the Footmen.

Of course, we are mindful that, on rare occasions, the ovens may fail and meals may be thus delayed. In such circumstances, the problem must be reported immediately, so that it may be fixed by the Estate Staff and the family is not unduly inconvenienced. The stock of cold meats must always be in satisfactory supply.

After dinner, when the most crucial part of the daily work is done, it is a good time to check on the contents of the larder and make sure everything is clean and tidily stored in the correct place.

PUNCTUALITY

The Cook sets the example for the rest of the kitchen staff. As mentioned previously for all servants, early rising is important. This is of particular importance for the Cook, Assistant Cook and Kitchen Maids in order to perform the many tasks pertaining to the timely delivery of meals. Punctuality is imperative. It is an inescapable truth that late arrival in the morning may jeopardise the timely delivery of dinner in the evening. The Cook should be woken with a tea tray by an appointed Kitchen Maid.

RECEIPTS

The Cook will keep detailed notes of favoured receipts for reference and so that the Assistant Cook and Kitchen Maids may also learn how to make the dishes.

ASSISTANT COOK & KITCHEN MAID

The Assistant Cook at Downton will work to the rule of the Cook, learning from her and helping with food preparation as instructed. The Kitchen Maids meanwhile take on most of the cleaning tasks to allow the Assistant Cook to attend to food preparation, but they shall also help with food preparation when required to do so by the Cook or Assistant Cook.

The Kitchen Maids shall keep the kitchen, larder, scullery and adjoining areas clean to ensure good hygiene and health for the whole household. All these areas must be thoroughly scoured twice a week, along with the table, shelves and cupboards. Cooking utensils must also be kept scrupulously clean for use throughout the day.

She is also required to prepare all manner of meat, fish and vegetables as instructed by the Cook.

EARLY-MORNING DUTIES OF A KITCHEN MAID

A Kitchen Maid will need to be the earliest in the house to rise, at 4.30am. She shall get dressed in clean, working clothes (a simple dress and apron is appropriate) and then go downstairs.

By now, the Hall Boy will have delivered the kindling wood and coal to the scuttles, so collect it in your basket along with matches, paper, brushes and blacking. Then go about the family bedrooms to light their fires, taking care to be quiet and not awake the inhabitants, returning to refill your basket as necessary.

In lighting the fire, take care to set the fire back from the grate to prevent the first smoke puffing out into the room.

You should then return to the kitchen to blacken the stove and lay the table for breakfast in the servants' hall. Additionally, prepare the daily supply of cooking salt, by rubbing a large block of solid salt through a sieve.

At 6am, knock on the bedroom doors of the Housemaids to wake them, before attending to the fires in the ground floor rooms – they must be prepared and lit in the libraries, drawing room, dining room and great hall. Unless it is winter or the weather is particularly cold, it is advantageous to open the windows a little before lighting the fires in general rooms, as this will create a draught, pushing the smoke up the chimney.

These tasks must be completed before the family or guests descend from their rooms, by which time you will have returned downstairs to assist with final breakfast preparations if required.

WASHING UP

The Kitchen Maid must not allow dirty plates, bowls and other utensils on tables when meals are being prepared. Take them to the scullery for washing up. There, rinse all non-greasy items immediately (this will make your job easier later) and leave them to drain by the sink.

The draining board slopes slightly towards the sink, so the easiest way to rinse cutlery is to place it there side by side and pour a jug of hot water over it. Rinse plates individually.

Return to wash items thoroughly as soon as possible between your cookery tasks then return them to their proper places.

After meals are served to the family, you must also make sure all pots and pans are scrubbed and cleaned ready for preparation of the next meal. Once the family have finished their meals and left the dining room, the Footmen will bring down the crockery and cutlery for you to wash.

Glass and china services used in the dining room by the family will be washed up by the Footmen and Hall Boys in the Servery under the guidance and direction of the Under Butler.

CLEANING PEWTER

Mix whiting with methylated spirits in equal proportion to make a thick paste, the consistency of double cream. Apply a small amount with a cloth to the pewter item, and rub in hard with another clean cloth. Finally, apply a chamois leather cloth for extra shine.

Wash and rinse utensils used for eating before storing away.

CLEANING COPPER POTS AND PANS

Mix a cupful of silver sand with a cupful of malt vinegar plus a little salt and flour to make a smooth paste. Rub on to the copper by hand and use a cloth to buff to a high shine.

INSTRUCTIONS FOR DAILY CLEANING
OF THE LARDER

~ Make sure all food is covered before cleaning.

~ Wipe shelves with a cloth using hot, soaped water.

~ Do not use a broom in the larder as it will only serve to excite dust – instead use a scrubbing brush and hot, soaped water.

~ Leave the door open after cleaning to let the air flow freely and assist drying.

FOOD PREPARATION

With three meals plus elevenses and tea for the family and servants' meals to prepare each day, there is much to be done and the Assistant Cook will be at the Cook's service to aid in all tasks as directed.

Be extremely vigilant: Footmen are prone to leaving their cleaning things lying around. It wouldn't do for a bowl of highly toxic salt of sorrel – used for cleaning brass – rather than chopped egg to be served for breakfast!

BREAKS

The kitchen staff will take breakfast after completing their early-morning duties and before the family come down from their bedrooms or whenever the Cook directs.

Again, lunch may be taken when directed at a time that it is convenient to do so by the Cook in a break suitable to the preparation of food for above and below stairs.

All servants have tea-break at 6.30pm, subject to the needs of the family and guests being satisfied. The sound of the dressing gong – when the family repair to their rooms to get dressed for dinner – marks the end of this break, when you shall return to kitchen duties as directed by the Cook.

The Cook will make the judgement over when the Kitchen Staff eat their supper. With the day's work done, servants are liable to linger awhile and socialise, but for the Kitchen Maid's benefit, the Cook will likely instruct them to go to bed once they have finished their food so they are well-rested for the following day's endeavours.

The Kitchen Maid shall also be entitled to a half-day off per week, as agreed with the Cook.

USEFUL NOTES FOR ALL
KITCHEN STAFF

APPEARANCE, DRESS & CLEANLINESS

Neatness of appearance is expected. Well-fitting shoes are a necessity. A plentiful supply of freshly-laundered aprons is available from the store cupboard so you should never be unduly dirty.

Fingernails must be kept short and particular attention must be paid to keeping hands clean at all times.

LOOSENING GLASS STOPPERS

Pour a little salad oil around the stopper and place the bottle close to the fire. Tap the stopper gently and the warmed oil shall loosen it.

A METHOD TO KILL FLIES IN THE KITCHEN
WITHOUT POISON

Mix one pint of milk with a quarter pound of sugar and two ounces of ground pepper, and then simmer for eight-to-ten minutes. Place in shallow saucers and the flies will attack it and be suffocated momentarily.

FUEL ECONOMY

There are some simple steps that can be taken to see that fuel is not burnt wastefully:

~ Only turn on as many burners as are necessary for the job in hand.

~ Mix a solution in the proportion of a handful of washing soda to 2 quarts of water and sprinkle on coal. Allow coal to dry before use and you will find the coal burns longer.

~ Don't keep water at boiling point when only a lower simmering temperature is required.

~ Sprinkle a mixture of ashes, coal dust and a little water on a coal fire and the fire will last longer.

ANT INVASIONS

Ants may quickly infest the kitchen (and general household) unless swiftly dealt with. An ant trail will lead back to the nest. When found, pour boiling water onto the nest.

THE AVOIDANCE OF WASTE

While we are most fortunate at Downton Abbey to have abundant productive land for our subsistence, the War has reminded us that nothing should be taken for granted and, in the kitchen, nothing should be wasted. This again requires imagination and good organisation. Each morning, check the larder for items that are soon to spoil and find a use for them. Crusts cut off bread used for sandwiches at afternoon tea may be dried in the oven for crumbing; when whites of eggs are needed for one purpose ensure that the yolk is also used for another purpose &c.

MRS BEETON'S

KITCHEN MAXIMS

A copy of *Mrs Beeton's All-About Cookery* book is always to hand in the kitchen with over 2,000 receipts to complement and inspire your own creations. Mrs Beeton also has some simple maxims for kitchen staff of all levels to commit to memory, some of which bear repeating here:

'A good manager looks ahead.'

'Clear as you go: muddle makes more muddle.'

'Dirty saucepans filled with hot water begin to clean themselves.'

'Thrust an oniony knife into the earth to take away the smell.'

'Search for insects in greens before putting them in to soak.'

'Green vegetables should be boiled fast with lid off.'

'Water boils when it gallops, oil when it is still.'

'When pastry comes out of the oven, meat may go in.'

'Fish boiled should be done slowly with a little vinegar in the water.'

'A stew boiled is a stew spoiled.'

'Pour boiling water over frying fat to clarify it, and set it aside for using again.'

'Make mint sauce two hours before serving it.'

'Salt or cold water makes scum to rise.'

'Scum as it rises in boiling should be taken off.'

'Always save the liquor in which a joint of meat has boiled.'

'Boiled puddings should fill the basin.'

'Pour nothing but water down the sink.'

However, remember that Mrs Beeton's words are a guide only and the Cook's guidance takes the lead.

PRESERVING & PICKLING

Here are outlined techniques to preserve and pickle for extended storage and good flavour.

Preserved Windsor beans

Gather the beans when barely half-grown. Procure pint-size preserve tin boxes and flat top lids from the storage cupboard, and fill them with the fresh beans and a sprig of winter savoury herbs. Add half a gill of water and a teaspoonful of salt, then solder down the tops.

Put the boxes in a stock-pot, fill near brimful with boiling water, boil fast for half an hour on the stove, and then withdraw.

Allow to cool fully and check for any leaks and solder afresh any that require it. Place in the cellar. Add a sprig of green winter savoury to each box of beans.

Preserved truffles

English truffles are at their best in winter around the turn of the new year, and cost a fraction of the French equivalent. It is therefore prudent to preserve quantities of this delicacy for use at special occasions throughout the year. The best means to do so is to attend to the following process:

- Thoroughly wash all dirt and grit from the truffles, and then peel them very thinly.
- Put them in bottles with wide necks.
- Add a tablespoonful of water, a saltspoonful of salt and a healthy sprig of thyme to each bottle.
- Cork tight, and secure down with wire or string.
- Boil for half an hour.
- Remove from the heat and cool.
- When cold, wax over the corks.

Ladies' Delight

Put eight ounces of chopped apples and the same of chopped onions and two ounces of chopped chillies into a jar. Boil one pint of white-wine vinegar with a dessertspoonful of salt and pour it into the jar. Mix and, when cold, use the pickle to be eaten with cold meats &c.

FOOTMAN

A Footman shall spend substantial time upstairs, in contact with family and guests, so his deportment must be as impeccable as his livery.

DUTIES

To include:

~ Laying the table for breakfast, lunch and supper.

~ Taking the dishes up from the kitchens and waiting the table (wear white gloves so as not to leave fingermarks on the plates or glasses).

~ Serving wine in the correct manner as taught by the Butler and Under Butler.

~ Clearing tables.

~ In between meals, attending to fires and helping serve tea in the library or drawing room.

~ Cleaning fine glassware as directed by the Butler.

~ Opening and closing doors.

~ Taking and delivering notes and messages.

~ Acting as Valet to any visitors who come without their own servants.

~ When travelling in a car with family or guests, sitting in the front with the chauffeur, ready to open the door and help passengers in or out.

One Footman shall be assigned responsibility each day for walking Lord Grantham's dog, first thing in the morning and last thing at night.

It is also useful to know how to dismantle, clean and reload a shotgun of any bore in case you are required as a loader on shoots. If you are not familiar in how to do this, you shall receive appropriate training.

POSTURE

A Footman's posture should be straight backed with the head held firmly upright and the neck in the back of the collar, not lolling to the sides, nor forward or back. Stand with your heels together and your feet at 45 degrees, and keep your shoulders down and relaxed. Hands should never be held in front – thumbs are aligned with the seams of your trousers.

It is good to maintain these habits when off-duty and not to slouch, so that good posture becomes second nature. Being relaxed in your stance when in service is important as you are expected to stand still without fidgeting for long periods.

THE QUIETEST WAY TO OPEN
AND CLOSE A DOOR

A good Footman moves around the household so quietly as to be inconspicuous, and the following method for opening and closing a door, while not essential, can greatly assist you in achieving this.

When opening a door and going through yourself, turn the handle and pass through the doorway keeping the handle turned. When you have passed through, take hold of the handle on the opposite side of the door with your other hand, and hold the catch open until you have gently closed the door, whereupon you can smoothly click the catch into place.

When opening the door for others, simply maintain hold of the handle on the near side of the door as they pass through before closing gently as above.

ACCOMPANYING LADIES

When you are asked to accompany ladies of the house as they visit friends or go shopping, you should be as immaculate in your dress as you are within the house. If walking, keep a respectful distance of two or three yards behind them. Your presence is to protect them from intrusion, insult or danger. If they require to cross a public street, check that it is safe for them to do so.

Should you be aware of the house that they are going to, when near, move ahead of them when you are twenty yards away and knock at the door so that it might be opened by the time they arrive.

Observe the same decorum when they are shopping, stepping forward to open the door for them, then close it again and wait outside for them. Stay alert so you are ready to open the door for them when they wish to leave.

RULES FOR WAITING AT THE
DINING ROOM TABLE

~ A Footman must always wear gloves when serving.

~ The Footmen will stand with their backs to the fireplace, facing the table.

~ Tread lightly at all times and be unhurried and discreet in all your actions in the dining room. The art of serving well is to be so unobtrusive that your presence is hardly noticed.

~ Never speak unless spoken to. If addressed, reply in a modest tone. Communicate with the Butler and fellow Footmen by gestures and leave the dining room and go below stairs if discussion is needed.

~ In bringing things up to the dining room, be careful to take a firm step on the stairs.

~ Ensure plates and cutlery are perfectly clean and dry when laying the table.

~ Always walk around the table in a clockwise direction.

~ Always serve items with the left hand, and from the left side of the person being served.

~ Never reach across the table or, when serving one diner, put your arm in front of another. Always be vigilant and certain not to tread on a lady's gown.

~ If any food from a dish falls on the table, remove it swiftly with a spoon and without inconveniencing diners by leaning over them.

~ Any spillage of food onto the table should be immediately cleaned off. On polished wood this should be done with a napkin, or a damp cloth and napkin. On a white table cloth a knife and napkin should solve the issue.

~ When removing plates and dishes, do so with great care so as to avoid spillage.

~ The Butler will signal when to clear each course; this will be when everyone eating has finished or on the instruction of Lady Grantham. Family and guests will indicate that they have finished by placing their knife and fork on the plate, fork to the left and knife, with blade facing left, to the right. The two will be points uppermost towards 12 o'clock on the plate, with their handles resting on the rim of the plate at 6 o'clock.

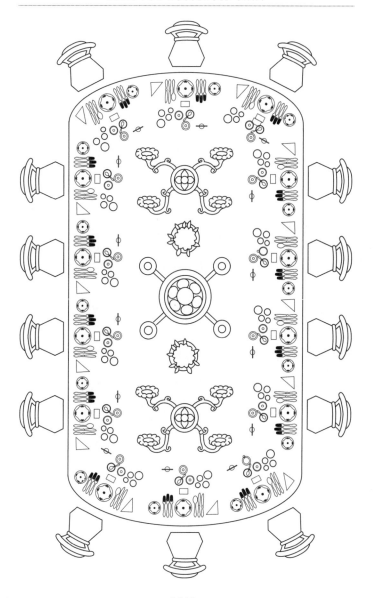

PRESENTATION OF NEWSPAPERS

When the newspapers for family and guests are delivered in the morning, they must be first be ironed with a warm iron. Press the front and the back pages with the iron, working from top to bottom of the page.

Clip the top and bottom of the centre page so that none of the pages fall out, and place them neatly on the sideboard in the dining room.

Please note: Lord Grantham takes *The Times* while her Ladyship prefers *The Sketch* which she will receive with breakfast in her room.

All newspapers must be kept pristine for reading throughout the day, so re-iron if necessary. They should be laid, after breakfast, in the library.

PARTICULAR INSTRUCTIONS FOR BREAKFAST SERVICE

First lay the linen cloth carefully on the table so as not to rumple it. Set a plate and knife and fork, where each person sits. Let there be sufficient tea cups and saucers and a teaspoon for each. Likewise if boiled eggs are to be served, provide enough egg cups and spoons for each person. If there are two kinds of butter, have two butter knives &c.

Place the cups and saucers so that they are conveniently to hand. Position the teapot, cream jug and slop basin behind the cups and saucers. The urn is placed on a rug behind the teapot.

Spread a tablecloth on the side-table, and place the meat and fish there together with carving knives and forks, mustard, salt and any other relishes.

How to make toast

If a diner desires toast dry, cut it thin and toast it in advance of it being served. Should they prefer it thick and moist, do not toast it until it is absolutely required.

How to make tea

Pour half a pint of boiling water into the empty teapot. Leave for two minutes and then pour out into the slop basin. Immediately put the tea in and close the lid so that the steam may penetrate the leaves. At the end of two minutes, add a half pint of boiling – and never less than boiling – water. When the liquid has stood for three minutes, top up with more boiling water and serve.

AFTERNOON TEA

When afternoon tea is served and a good number of people are present, normally two Footmen will stand at either side of the Butler at the table. You will be on hand to return to the kitchen to refill the tea urn and replenish the sandwiches and cakes as required, and to do whatsoever the Butler instructs to please the family and guests.

ADVICE FOR DINNER SERVICE

The Under Butler will train you thoroughly in all aspects of laying the table and service, probably during your time as a Hall Boy, but here follows some useful principles and advice to keep in mind:

~ The Footman lays the cloth, cutlery and glasses with the Under Butler ensuring that they are correctly laid out to his plan and adding the silver articles.

~ The silver will be collected from the strong room and signed out of the Inventory Book under the supervision of the Butler. The silver will then be carried up to the dining room and placed in accordance with the Dining Room Table Book by Footmen in silver handling gloves, if necessary standing on the table in special footwear to protect the surface, under the direction of the Under Butler.

~ The long table in the Downton Abbey dining room can comfortably seat twenty people, with one or two at each end. Before laying the cutlery, first place the chairs around the table, so that diners on each side are directly opposite each other and have enough elbow room to eat without inconveniencing their neighbour. Lord and Lady Grantham's chairs are to be opposite each other in the middle between the fire and central windows.

When there are fewer people for dinner a smaller table should be employed. If there are just four people for breakfast for example, use the smallest table by removing all the leaves.

~ Place baize under the tablecloth to both protect the table and hold the cloth in place. Make sure the centre crease of the tablecloth is at the centre of table and that the overhang is even on all sides.

~ The spoons and knives are placed on the right of the place setting and the forks on the left, and the guest will know to start with the outside utensils and move inwards with each course.

~ A handwritten menu – in French always, unless there is one word that can't be translated, in which case the menu is entirely in English – is placed above the cutlery, centred between the cutlery left and right, and in line horizontally with the first glass.

~ Make sure the salt, pepper and mustard (French) are within easy reach of each person, ideally with one set each.

~ It is always well to have extra serving spoons and forks within reach in the dining room. Then if a guest places a serving spoon back in the wrong dish, leaving the dish from whence it came spoon-less, simply supply a clean spoon rather than retrieve the misplaced one.

~ The Butler will inform Lady Grantham with a look when dinner is ready. She will be among family and guests gathered in the drawing room.

~ When the family and guests have left the dining room, extinguish the candles on the table. Blowing them out will likely get wax on the tablecloth and create extra cleaning work, so it is best to squeeze the flame with the fingers, being sure to wet them first to avoid burning.

THE CORRECT WORDING FOR PLACE CARDS*

TITLE	PLACE CARD
The Sovereign	*The King*
Queen Mary	*The Queen*
The Prince of Wales	*The Prince of Wales*
Royal Duke	*The Duke of York*
Princess Mary	*The Princess Royal*
Duke/Duchess	*The Duke/Duchess of Norfolk*
Son of a Duke or Marquess	*The Lord Henry Cholmondeley*
Daughter of a Duke, Marquess or Earl	*The Lady Constance Cholmondeley*
Widow of a Duke	*The Dowager Duchess of Northumberland*
Marquess/Marchioness	*The Marquess/Marchioness of Winchester*
Widow of a Marquess	*The Dowager Marchioness of Winchester*
Earl/Countess	*The Earl/Countess of Elgin*
Son of an Earl, Viscount or Baron	*Mr Victor Bruce*
Widow of an Earl	*The Dowager Countess of Elgin*
Viscount/Viscountess	*The Viscount/Viscountess Ullswater*
Daughter of a Viscount or Baron	*Miss Celia Grey*

Widow of a Viscount	*The Dowager Viscountess Ullswater*
Widow of a Baron	*The Dowager Lady Grey*
Baronet	*Sir John Smith*
Wife of a Baronet	*Lady Smith*
Widow of a Baronet	*Ursula, Lady Smith*
Knight	*Sir Andrew North*
Wife of a Knight	*Lady North*
Dame Grand Cross or Dame Commander	*Dame Constance Elms*
Husband of a Dame	*Mr David Elms*
Gentleman	*Mr David Stratham*
Gentleman's wife	*Mrs David Stratham*
Unmarried woman	*Miss Erica Stratham*

Some Dowagers prefer to be referred to now by their first names before a comma, and then the title they held when married. For example, The Dowager Marchioness of Zetland might choose to be addressed as Harriet, Marchioness of Zetland.

Eldest sons of Dukes, Marquesses and Earls generally carry courtesy titles by which they are known. These are the titles of second rank to their parent. The eldest son of The Duke of Argyll is the Marquess of Lorne.

stated names and places are given for example only.

FOLDING NAPKINS

First, check that the napkins have been lightly starched and clean your hands thoroughly.

There are innumerable configurations in which napkins may be presented. More elaborate methods can render the napkin wrinkly, and therefore we lean towards more classical forms such as 'The Bishop's Hat' and 'The Crown Fold' (see below).

It is important to practise this and any other method you are shown, so that when you come to prepare the table you are able to swiftly and properly fold the napkins without mangling the cloth. Folds are made clean and crisp by pressing down with the palm or thumb. The side of the fist may be applied when a number of layers need to be dealt with at once.

The Crown Fold

1. Lay the napkin face-down and fold in half on the diagonal.

2. Turn the napkin so that the closed end is nearest to you.

3. Fold the right corner up so that the point rests directly on furthest corner and the edge of the new flap lies on the centre line of the napkin.

4. Repeat the same procedure on the left.

5. You should now have a diamond shape in front of you.

6. Fold the bottom of the napkin up as shown, so the point reaches up about two-thirds of the way to top corner. Press down firmly on the new fold.

7. Fold down the top of the smaller triangle so the point is aligned to the near edge. Press this fold down well.

8. Pick up the extreme left and right corners and curl them towards each other. When they meet in the middle, tuck one into the other.

9. Stand the napkin up, making sure the base is perfectly circular and that the flaps on either side are even.

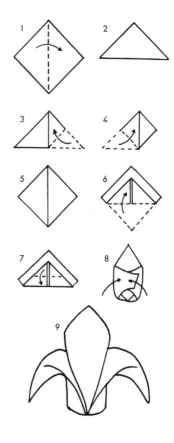

The Bishop's Hat

Note: to be used only for Sunday lunch

1. Lay the napkin face down.

2. Fold in half so that the open end is towards you.

3. Take the far-right corner and fold diagonally until the point rests in centre of the side nearest you.

4. Fold the near-left corner diagonally away until it rests next to the previous fold.

5. Flip the napkin over as shown.

6. Fold the bottom half of the napkin up and away from you, such that the far edges are in line.

7. Reach underneath and pull out the flap on the right to create two triangles.

8. Turn the left half of the triangle in and under the right triangle.

9. Flip the napkin over as shown.

10. Fold the right triangle to the left and tuck its end into the other triangle.

11. Open up the 'hat' and press down the cloth inside to fill out the circular shape.

12. Behold! The Bishop's Hat is ready to grace the table.

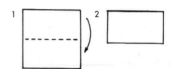

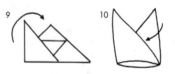

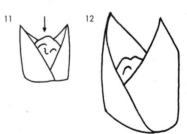

A PROPERLY POLISHED GLASS

There is a difference between a clean glass and a perfectly polished glass that is fit for service.

Hold a linen cloth in both hands and hold the base of the glass gently in your left hand. Now rotate the glass clockwise with your right hand, assisting this movement by your left hand moving anti-clockwise. Be careful not to apply too much pressure to the top of the glass as it could break. Turn a few times until it is perfectly polished.

Still holding the cloth, place the glass in its correct position, without allowing your fingers to touch it – even the slightest contact will show on highly polished glass.

SERVING PLATES & DISHES CORRECTLY

Plates must be held with the fingers spread widely gripping the underside, and only the ball of the thumb resting against the side of the plate. The thumb should never intrude over the rim of a plate.

To hold a serving dish laden with food in the left hand while the diner serves requires some strength. This will be extremely taxing to the novice, but over time the wrist will strengthen and it will become easier. Keep the fingers and thumb well spread beneath the dish, and press the thumb and little fingers against either side of the under-rim to keep it steady.

Serve from the left of the person, putting your left foot forward, bending the knee and keeping the dish in line above your left foot for support. Bend the elbow to bring the dish down to a convenient height for the diner to help themself and close enough to the plate that food cannot fall from serving spoon or fork onto the table.

Before serving the next person, bring your right hand under the dish to relieve your left hand for a moment. This is particularly important for the inexperienced Footman, unused to carrying such weight. It is better to take a second or two of relief than drop the dish. Collect the serving spoon and fork then serve the next guest.

FINE CLEANING AND POLISHING OF
KNIVES & FORKS

To clean and polish cutlery to a shine after washing up, you will require a board covered with smooth leather. Spread a small amount of melted suet over the board with a flannel and then rub two pieces of Bath brick against each other, covering the board with brick dust until no grease comes through.

Then take a knife in each hand and put them flat against the leather and scour them by moving your arms to and from the body; when one side of a knife is done, turn over and repeat.

Take care not to press too hard on the blade, for a good steel knife is liable to snap.

To clean forks, put some fine sea sand or brick dust into an old flowerpot, or small barrel, mixed with a little slightly dampened hay or moss. Rubbing the fork several times into this will remove stains.

Then take a thin stick, or whalebone, wrapped in chamois leather, to polish the prongs and notches at the lower part of the knife blades.

Thorough cleaning of knives and forks shall ensure no rusty marks which will spoil their appearance. Should the family be going to the country, even greater care must be taken with these articles as you cannot always be on hand to inspect them.

Stains or yellowing to ivory handles may be removed by mixing a little water with a few drops of spirits of salt. Dip a flannel or soft sponge into it, rub the stain and it will instantly disappear.

CLEANING DECANTERS, JUGS &c.

Some cut-glass decanters are extremely valuable and must be handled with care. To clean, fill to half or three parts full with warm water (boiling water may crack the glass) and drop in some small pieces of brown paper that have been well soaped. Leave to soak for an hour or two, shaking well every now and then. Use a long-handled bottle brush to clean the crevices around the neck and bottom.

Decanters that have had port or other wine in them for some time will have crusty deposits therein. Add a little potash or soda to the warm water at first, let it remain a short while, shake well and then proceed as directed above.

When all dirt is removed, rinse thoroughly with clean, cold water, and place upside down on the draining rack.

Once dry, the outside of the glass may be polished. First, rub over with a damp cloth and whiting. Rub off the whiting with a dry cloth and a soft brush for the crevices, and polish bright with a chamois leather.

Decanters and jugs that are rarely used and not dried properly are prone to mildew. This will spoil the taste of anything put in them, so see to it that they are perfectly dry before putting away. And wrap a piece of paper around each stopper to prevent sticking.

When decanters are put away with wine in them, put in corks and hang the stoppers round the neck of each decanter with a piece of string.

CLEANING PLATE SILVER

Plate silver items should be washed in hot, soapy water as soon as possible after being cleared from the table. Do not delay in washing them as it will double your work to remove encrusted grime.

Remove the items and wipe with a soft cloth, and then place in another bowl of hot water to which a tablespoonful of ammonia has been added. Take items out of this water and dry without draining them. Then rub carefully with chamois leather.

CORRECT STORAGE OF
EVERYDAY SILVER CUTLERY

Silver in everyday use is kept in soft-lined drawers with dividers in the servery. Make sure the knives, forks and spoons are all thoroughly cleaned and place them on their sides in the drawer – never stack, because silver can scratch easily.

CANDLESTICKS – CLEANING AND DISPLAY

Great care must be taken in cleaning silver and plated candlesticks to avoid the risk of scratching in removing the wax or grease. Do not, then, use a knife for this purpose or hold the candlestick near the fire to melt the wax.

The best method to remove the wax or grease without injury to the object is to pour boiling water on it and then wipe clean with an old cloth.

The exception is for Japanned candlesticks, on which boiling water must never be poured as the varnish shall crack, or candlesticks with glass. Instead, use warm water, just hot enough to melt the grease, then wipe them with a cloth. If smears remain, sprinkle on a little flour and then rub it clean.

Always have the candles set up in the morning ready, including the hand candles which may be required to seal a letter.

Before setting, always light the candles to burn off the cotton.

To place the candle, put the finger and thumb of your right hand at the top of the candle and press down firmly into the socket, observing that it is perfectly upright. For candlesticks with several branches a keen eye for perpendicularity is of particular significance.

If you discover the sockets are too large for the candle, wrap paper around the end to fill out, but ensure that none is visible above the socket. If the candle is too broad, scrape the base carefully that it may be put in far enough not to endanger it falling out when the candlestick is moved.

If the dirtying or yellowing of the candle wax should be seen, apply a piece of flannel dipped in wine spirits, which will make them look well again.

The correct method for uncorking champagne

The seemingly simple task of uncorking a bottle of champagne carries great potential for embarrassment. The French seem oblivious to such concerns with their penchant for *sabrage*, holding the bottle at arm's length and swiping off the neck just under the cork and sending champagne cascading everywhere.

Follow this method to avoid such indignities:

1. Cut the wire at the rim of the bottle and then remove each string in the same way.

2. Hold the cork down with the left thumb and use a penknife to scrape away any dirt which may have accumulated between the overlapping cork and the rim, a particular problem with older bottles.

3. Extract the cork very slowly so that it makes no noise on its release, and have a glass to hand in case the wine is lively and bubbles forth.

4. Wait for the liquid to settle and only serve when the wine flows out steadily.

5. Fill a champagne glass to about a quarter of an inch from the brim.

6. Refill half-empty glasses to this level as required, but be wary of refilling too often lest you encourage excessive consumption.

THE CORRECT METHOD FOR SERVING WINE

From the bottle

Pick up the bottle with one hand with the label away from you – this way, if someone asks what wine you are serving, you can easily show them the label. The forefinger is pressed firmly down on the shoulder of the bottle, with the thumb below the shoulder and at angle clasping the other side of the bottle. This positioning will allow you to walk around the table without altering your grip and to pour smoothly and with control.

Always serve from the right of the person. Place your right foot slightly in front of your left so that is under the table, then pour into the glass until it is no more than three-quarters full (or less, if asked). Before withdrawing the bottle, give it a gentle flick to ensure any wine on the lip of the bottle drops into the glass rather than down the bottle and onto the table.

As you move onto the next person, hold the bottle upright, close to your ribcage.

From the decanter

At Downton, we normally use a crystal glass decanter with a handle, which makes handling and pouring simple. If you are called upon to use a decanter without a handle, grasp it firmly around the neck, just beneath the lip, so that it is ready to pour.

When serving both from the bottle and a decanter (without handle) at the same time, hold the bottle in the left hand and the decanter in the right for more control. In this case, of course, you will have to step forward with your left leg to serve the wine in your left hand.

Serving port, brandy and liqueurs

After dinner, the ladies will retire to the drawing room and the gentlemen will remain in the dining room for port, brandy &c. and to smoke cigars. Always serve from the right-hand side of the person. Once all of those present have been served, replace the stopper in the decanter (or decanters) and leave it on right-hand side of his Lordship before leaving the room.

It is important to replace the stopper in decanters of liqueurs because such full-bodied fortified wines easily absorb the odours in the air. Smoke will affect the flavour of a port wine, for example, such that non-smokers can taste the difference.

FIRST AID

Intoxication

Neither beer, wine nor spirits are of themselves harmful unless drunk to excess, but the effects of intoxication can be fatal. If one encounters a gentleman – we shall assume it is not a lady, perish the thought – in a state of intoxication he should be left alone until his clothes have been loosened and body laid on his belly, the posture most favourable for continuing vital breathing motions, discharging the contents of the stomach &c. Then lay him on his side with particular care taken that his neck is in no way twisted or tight.

Note that it can be of fatal consequence for a person to attempt to quench their excessive degree of thirst occasioned by drinking strong acid liquor, by drinking freely of milk. It is safest after a debauch to prescribe water with a slice of toast, infusions of balm, sage, barley water and the like.

If the patient requires to vomit in order to evacuate the intoxicants, a mixture of lukewarm water and oil will do it, or simply tickling the throat with a finger or a feather.

The following day, administering a morsel of boiled beef well salted or a slice of red herring is advised to settle the stomach.

Fainting

In fainting fits of any kind, fresh air is always of greatest importance. Hence, do not allow people to crowd round the patient as this is dangerous.

When a person faints from drinking, fullness of blood, vigorous exercise, intense study or the like, a whiff of vinegar shall help to bring them round. Also mix vinegar in an equal quantity of warm water and apply with a flannel to the temples, forehead and wrists. As the person begins to revive, if they are able to swallow, two spoonfuls of vinegar mixed with five times as much cold water may be poured into their mouth.

More often, swoonings are due to heat, want of water and lack of appetite. In such case a directly opposite approach should be taken.

(continues)

Lay the patient in bed, rub their whole body strongly with hot flannels, lay hot water bottles at the feet and apply a compress of flannel dipped in hot brandy to the stomach. Smelling salts or pungent herbs such as rosemary or mint may be held to the nose. Wet the mouth with a little rum or brandy, and when the invalid is ready to swallow, hot wine mixed with sugar and cinnamon may be poured into their mouth.

Strong broth or a little bread soaked in hot-spiced wine will help to speed their recovery thereafter.

MEDICINAL DRINKS

Lime-flower Tea

For indigestion, hysteria and anti-spasmodic qualities
Pour one pint of boiling water upon half an ounce of lime-flowers. Allow to stand for ten minutes, pour into a cup, sweeten with honey and it is ready to drink.

Marshmallow water

For inveterate coughs, catarrhs &c.
Soak one ounce of marshmallow roots in a little cold water for half an hour. Remove and peel off the bark. Cut the roots into thin shavings and place in a jug. Add a pint of boiling water, and allow to infuse for two to three hours.

The liquor is drunk tepid, and may be sweetened with honey or sugar-candy, or flavoured with orange juice.

Dandelion Tea

For biliousness and the treatment of dropsy
Add one ounce of dandelion to a pint of boiling water and continue to boil for ten minutes. Remove from the heat, decant the mixture into a jug, sweeten with honey and drink a small glassful at regular intervals through the day.

Violet Tea

For relief of pain, bronchitis attacks, fever, chronic catarrh &c.
Infuse one teaspoonful of dried violets in half a pint of boiling water for five minutes. Sweeten with honey. May be drunk hot or cold.

Hop Tea

To improve appetite and strengthen the digestive organs
Put half an ounce of hops into a jug with a lid. Pour a pint of boiling water on the hops and close the lid. Allow the hops to infuse the water until the mixture is quite cold. Decant the mixture into another jug or bottle and drink when fasting.

CURATIVES

A gargle for sore throat

Mix a small glass of port wine, a tablespoonful of chilli vinegar, six sage leaves and a dessertspoonful of honey. Simmer for five minutes and gargle when still warm.

A cure for the sting of wasps or bees

A bruised leaf of poppy applied to the affected part will offer immediate relief from a sting.

A cure for warts

Add a few drops of reduced vinegar to the bruised leaves of the marigold (calendula officinalis) and apply to the wart, morning and night.

Relief for sprains

Bruise a handful of sage leaves and boil them in vinegar for five minutes. Apply to the affected area with a napkin as hot as can be borne by the afflicted person.

Relief for burns

Crush an onion and a potato in a mortar, add a tablespoonful of salad oil, and mix well. Apply to the burn and secure with a bandage.

A cure for chapped hands

Add one and a half ounces of olive oil to one ounce of spermaceti, one ounce of virgin wax, one ounce of camphor and two ounces of honey in a basin. Cover the basin and place in a stew pan containing a little hot water, then set close to the fire. When dissolved, stir together well. Wait until it is quite cold before use.

HOUSEMAID

Housemaids are responsible for the general cleanliness and tidiness of the household. A good Maid will pay close attention to the instructions and example of the Housekeeper and follow the direction of any Maid that is her senior. She should take great pride in contributing to the immaculate presentation of each room she attends to.

Uniforms are provided – day dresses for cleaning, and black evening dresses which should be worn after the duties of the afternoon and before the dining gong. They must be worn by any Maid assisting with the preparation of family tea.

Tasks will be allotted each day by the Housekeeper and passed on through the senior House Maids, including:

~ Making sure the curtains, ornaments and flowers are in good order.

~ Sweeping, dusting and polishing.

~ Cleaning looking-glasses.

~ Straightening newspapers and magazines.

~ Plumping cushions and beating rugs.

~ Making beds and changing sheets in the bedroom before breakfast, refilling biscuit jars, refreshing water jugs &c.

~ Folding the towels and cleaning the washbasins in the cloakrooms.

When cleaning the rooms in the morning, before the family get up, the head Housemaid is expected to carry out the most delicate tasks, such as dusting valuable objects and fine furniture.

APPROVED METHODS

For sweeping

In Downton Abbey which is free from the dirt and grime of the city, there is less dust to contend with, so it is not necessary to sweep carpets every day. Once a week is sufficient in lesser used rooms and twice in those more often occupied. However, it is the style of the house that during luncheon, tea and dinner we brush all the carpets of the rooms that the family have been using and have temporarily vacated.

Always keep at hand dust sheets to cover sofas, book cases &c. as sweeping will kick up dust. To reduce the spread of dust, the kitchen staff will always keep the used tea leaves from the family table. When dampened and sprinkled on the carpet, the leaves will collect the dust. Sweep them up, carry away in a dust pan and dispose of in the ash hole.

Make sure to sweep scrupulously the darkest recesses and under furniture – in less well-maintained houses the carpet will appear a different colour under the piano or sofa for want of proper brushing.

Sweep first before cleaning and polishing the furniture and ornaments.

To make furniture polish

An excellent protective polish for furniture may be made using the following ingredients:

2oz beeswax

1 tablespoon of wine vinegar

1 dessertspoon of turpentine

Place the beeswax in an enamelled bowl, put the bowl in a saucepan of hot water over a low heat, and stir. As the hard beeswax starts to melt, add the turpentine (exercise great care in doing so, as turpentine is highly flammable). Mix well and then add the wine vinegar, continuing to stir steadily so as to avoid dangerous splashes.

Once the mixture is smooth, pour into a labelled jar. Cover securely so that it is air-tight and then store in a cool, dry place, ready for use.

To make floor polish, slowly melt half a pound of beeswax over a low heat in the same way. Once melted, remove from the heat and thoroughly mix in a pint and a half of turpentine. Pour the mixture into a labelled jar, seal and store.

Cloths and polishing

You will need three cloths to hand for wax polishing: one to apply the polish, one to work the polish into the surface until it is no longer sticky and one to buff in a circular motion to a high shine.

As we polish regularly at Downton, it shall only be necessary to apply a small amount of polish each time.

The cloths used should be as soft as possible so as not to injure the furniture – silk or soft wool are best. A good, soft cloth is invaluable, but will blacken quickly if not looked after, so wash after every second use.

Dusting cloths must also be kept soft so that they can polish surfaces as delicate as glass. As your last duty of each day, wash dusters in soapy water, rinse thoroughly and leave to dry naturally overnight.

To remove ink stains from mahogany

If the spot has been made recently, rubbing it with a damp, soaped cloth may be enough to remove the mark. However, if it has been there some time and is more stubborn, rub it with soft cork while wet to lift up all the ink that is moveable. Then wipe off the soap and while the spot is wet drop a little diluted spirit of salts on it. Leave for a minute to allow the acidity to take effect and then wipe off with clean water and a cloth. If any ink still remains, repeat the last step. Once the spot has been removed, polish as normal.

To restore cut flowers

Fresh flowers will begin to droop and fade after a day or so, but many may be revived by the use of hot water. Immerse in scalding hot water high enough to cover about a third of the stems. When the water has cooled, the flowers will again be fresh and erect. Cut off the boiled ends and transfer to cold water and a smaller vase.

To clean looking glasses

Great care must be taken so as to avoid cracking the glass or damaging the frame. Some of our looking glasses are very large and you will require steps to reach them, in which case, make sure that the steps are firmly placed and you are not obliged to lean against the glass for support.

First, rub over the glass in a circular motion with a piece of soft chamois leather that has been dipped in clean water and wrung almost dry. Then rub the glass completely dry with a clean, soft cloth.

If the glass appears at all greasy after applying the chamois, follow up by dusting with dry powdered whiting or powdered blue tied in muslin, and then finish with dry cloths as before.

The smoke of candles can make looking-glasses particularly greasy and for this it is recommended to wet a sponge, squeeze dry and then dip it in spirits of wine as a first step, with whiting or powdered blue and cloths for finishing.

Clean very large chimney-glasses in stages, wetting only so much as can be conveniently cleaned before it gets dry or it will not look bright.

In all cases, quick and light rubbing is the order of the day, and take care not to touch the gilt frame with the damp sponge or leather. Frames should be dusted very delicately with a soft brush or feather duster, and not even rubbed with dry cloth. If any dirt is found, it may be lightly rubbed off with cotton wool without injuring the frame.

To clean picture frames

Use the same methods as above to clean picture frames and the glass over framed prints. However, never attempt to clean oil paintings – there are many valuable oil paintings at Downton and a specialist is always employed to attend to these. All you are expected to do is keep the pictures and frames free from dust using a feather brush.

Before the summer season, we cover the gilt frames of pictures and looking glasses with tissue paper to protect them from flies and dust. In carrying out this task, however, take care not to injure the walls or scratch the frames with the pins used to secure the paper.

To clean wallpaper

First blow away all the dust with a pair of bellows. Then cut a stale loaf of bread into pieces that will fit comfortably into your hand. Take one crust in hand and beginning with the ceiling, wipe the paper lightly downward about half a yard at each sweeping stroke. Take care not to rub the paper hard or in a horizontal direction. Continue across the room until the upper part of the paper is cleaned all round one side of the room. Then go again, this time beginning each downward stroke a little higher up than where the first extended to. Continue until the whole wall is finished.

Cut the dirty part of the bread away as you go, and take a new piece as and when the crumb is worn away.

If properly performed, this operation will frequently make old unvarnished paper appear as good as new.

For rooms with varnished paper, clean with a sponge with soapy cold water and wipe dry with a clean cloth.

To clean stone stairs and halls

Boil a pound of pipemaker's clay with a quart of water and a quart of small-beer and add a little stone-blue. Wash the stone with this mixture and, when dry, rub the stones with a flannel and brush.

To prevent fire irons from rusting

Smear melted mutton suet over the iron while hot. Then dust it well with unslacked lime pounded and tied up in a muslin.

Fire irons should be wrapped in baize and kept in a dry place when not in use.

To blacken the fronts of stone chimney pieces

Mix some oil varnish with lamp-black and a little spirits of turpentine to a paint-like consistency. Wash the stone with soapy water and then sponge with clear water. Once dry, brush the stone over with the blackening mixture. Repeat once.

To clean blankets

With new blankets, place in water to which borax has been added – soaking for a short time will neutralise the acid in the material. Then wash in warm soapy water, rinse carefully, put through the wringer and hang dry.

To make the beds and tidy bedrooms

If the weather is fine and temperature moderate or better, open the windows to air the room on entering. Remember to close them when you have finished your work.

The bed mattress should be turned every week, so it is necessary to work in pairs to attend to this heavy task. Remove the eiderdown and either air downstairs in the linen room, or fold and place in the bottom drawer of the chest of drawers. Pillows too should be regularly taken downstairs to air, leaving the bolster cushions under the counterpane during the day. Shake every pillow and bolster cushions well so that they are thoroughly aired and the feathers within well distributed. Neatly draw the bed curtains to their posts, straighten the bed carpets (and sweep the room if necessary, as above). The dressing rooms are the domain of the Valet or Lady's Maid, and you must not touch the dressing table, but speak with them to ask if there is anything they need you to deal with.

Check the windows for damp, dust and fly spots and rub clear and bright. If the sun is shining strongly close the blinds before leaving the room – carpets will quickly fade if exposed to too much sunlight.

To take mildew out of linen

Rub the affected areas well with soap and then scrape some fine chalk and rub into the linen. Allow to dry then repeat.

To dust books and bookcases correctly

Dust can damage book bindings, so regular dusting is essential.

Begin dusting on the top shelf and work downwards. Do not let the corners of your cloth flap about as this will only spread dust, defeating the objective of your work. When dusting each book, pay most attention to the spine and top edge where dust builds up.

First, remove four books at the end of the shelf to give you room to manoeuvre, and place carefully nearby. Dust the space left.

Push the books to the back of the bookcase, dust the front of the bookcase and then pull them to the front edge of the shelf again.

(Note: you will see that books are placed with their spines aligned at the front of the shelf rather than pressed against the back of the bookcase, so that the spines can be easily read. This is how they should replaced, and, of course, in the same order.)

Next, with your left hand, take hold of as many books as you can securely (a maximum of four) and tip them towards you at angle so you may dust the top of pages and the spines with your right hand.

Repeat the process until you reach the end of the shelf. Take the last book and dust its back cover as well as it has been exposed to dust.

Finally, dust the four books you earlier removed, including the cover of the first book on the shelf, and replace.

MODERN CLEANING PRODUCTS

Generally, we find traditional homemade cleaning agents to be best, but there are some alternative products now available which may be effectively employed:

Johnson's Polishing Wax

This wax can be applied to polish and preserve woodwork and items of furniture.

Zog

Cleans a variety of surfaces without scouring. Spinkle a little on a damp rag or mop as required and it can safely be applied to: paintwork; windows; glass & mirrors; baths; washbasins, brass and copper, silver and plate, tiles; sinks; china, porcelain enamel.

Silvo

May be applied to give a deep mirror-like polish to all kinds of silverware. Contains neither acid nor mercury so is safe for electro-plate as well.

APPENDIX

TABLE 1

Order of precedence among ladies, as a guide to the proper management of guests, the marshalling of table places and for servants to understand their respective ranks:

The Queen

Sovereign's daughters
Wife of the Heir Apparent
Wives of Sovereign's younger sons
Daughters of Sovereign's sons
Wives of Sovereign's Grandsons
Sovereign's sisters
Wives of Sovereign's brothers
Sovereign's aunts
Wives of Sovereign's uncles
Sovereign's nieces
Wives of Sovereign's nephews
Daughters of the Princess Royal, then of other Princesses
Duchesses (in the order of Dukes)
Wives of the eldest sons of the Dukes of the Blood Royal
Marchionesses (in the order of Marquesses)
Wives of the eldest sons of Dukes
Daughters of Dukes
Countesses (in the order of Earls)
Wives of younger sons of Dukes of the Blood Royal
Wives of the elder sons of Marquesses
Wives of younger sons of Dukes
Viscountesses (in the order of Viscounts)
Wives of the eldest sons of Earls
Daughters of Earls

Wives of younger sons of Marquesses
Baronesses (in the order of Barons)
Wives of the eldest sons of Viscounts
Wives of the younger sons of Earls
Wives of the elder sons of Barons
Daughters of Barons
Maids of Honour
Wives of the younger sons of Viscounts
Wives of the younger sons of Barons
Wives of Baronets (in the order of Baronets)
Dames Grand Cross of the Order of the British Empire
Wives of Knights Grand Cross (in order of their husbands' rank)
Dame Commanders of the Order of the British Empire
Wives of Knights (in order of their husbands' rank)
Commanders of the British Empire
Wives of the Companions and Commanders of the Order
Wives of Companions of the Distinguished Service Order
Officers of the British Empire
Wives of holders of the 4th Class of the Royal Victorian Order
    of the British Empire
Wives of Officers of the Order of the British Empire
Companions of the Imperial Service Order
Wives of Companions of the Imperial Service Order
Wives of the eldest sons of younger sons of Peers
Wives of the elder sons of Baronets
Daughters of Baronets
Wives of the elder sons of Knights
Daughters of Knights
Members of the Order of the British Empire
Wives of Members of the 5th Class of the Royal Victorian Order
Wives of Members of the Order of the British Empire
Wives of the younger sons of Peers' younger sons
Wives of the younger sons of Baronets and then of Knights
Wives of Esquires
Wives of Gentlemen

TABLE II

Order of precedence among gentlemen as a guide to the preparations of table plans, and for servants to understand their respective ranks:

The Sovereign

The Prince of Wales

Sovereign's younger sons

Sovereign's grandsons

Sovereign's brothers

Sovereign's uncles

Sovereign's nephews

Lord High Steward

Archbishop of Canterbury

Lord High Chancellor

Archbishop of York

Prime Minister and First Lord of the Treasury

Lord High Treasurer

Lord President of the Council

Speaker of the House of Commons

Lord Privy Seal

Lord Great Chamberlain (when on duty)

Earl Marshal

Lord High Admiral of the United Kingdom

Lord Steward of the Household

Lord Chamberlain of the Household

Master of the Horse

Dukes of England, Scotland, Great Britain, Ireland, United Kingdom and then Ireland after union

Eldest sons of Dukes of the Blood Royal

Marquesses of England, Scotland, Great Britain, Ireland, United Kingdom and then Ireland after 1800

Eldest sons of Dukes

Younger sons of Dukes of the Blood Royal

Marquesses eldest sons

Dukes' younger sons

Viscounts of England, Scotland, Great Britain, Ireland, United Kingdom
and then Ireland after 1800

Earls' eldest sons

Marquesses younger sons

Bishops of London, Durham and Winchester

Other Bishops, in order of consecration

Moderator of the General Assembly of the Church of Scotland

Secretaries of State, if Barons (Order: Home, Foreign, Colonial, War, India)

Barons of England, Scotland, Great Britain, Ireland, United Kingdom and
then Ireland after 1800

Treasurer of the Household

Comptroller of the Household

Vice Chamberlain of the Household

Secretaries of State below the rank of Baron

Viscounts eldest sons

Earls youngest sons

Barons eldest sons

Knights of the Garter, if not peers

Privy Counsellors, if not peers

Chancellor of the Exchequer

Chancellor of the Duchy of Lancaster

Lord Chief Justice

Master of the Rolls

Lord Justice of Appeal and President of Probate Courts

Judges in the High Court of Justice

Viscounts' younger sons

Sons of Lords of Appeal in Ordinary

Baronets

Knights of the Thistle

Knights of St Patrick

Knight Grand Cross of the Bath
Knights Grand Commander of the Star of India
Knights Grand Cross of St Michael and St George
Knights Grand Commander of the Indian Empire
Knight Grand Cross of the Royal Victorian Order
Knights Grand Cross of the Order of the British Empire
Second Class of Orders, in the above order
Knights Bachelor
Judges of Country Courts
Masters in Chancery
Masters in Lunacy
3rd Class of Orders, in the above order
Companions of the Distinguished Service Order
4th Class of the Royal Victorian Order and Order of the British Empire
Companions of the Imperial Service Order
Eldest sons of the younger sons of Peers
Eldest sons of Baronets
Eldest sons of Knights
5th Class of the Royal Victorian Order and the Order of the British Empire
Baronets' younger sons
Knights' younger sons
Esquires
Gentlemen

REFERENCES

A Butler's Guide to Entertaining
Nicholas Clayton, 2011, National Trust
Books

*A Modern System of Domestic Cookery or
The Housekeeper's Guide*
Radcliffe, M., 1824, J.Gleave & Son

Debretts.com

Francatelli's Cook's Guide
Charles Elmé Francatelli, 1884,
Bentley

*Home Sweet Home: The Best of Good
Housekeeping 1922–1939*
Compiled by Brian Braithwaite &
Noëlle Walsh, 1992, Ebury Press

Lowney's Cook Book
Maria Willet Howard, 1912 (Revised
Edition), The Walter M Lowney Co

Mrs Beeton's All-About Cookery, etc
Mrs Isabella Beeton, 1951 (New and
Revised Edition), Ward, Lock &
Co. Ltd

Napkinfoldingguide.com

The Book of Household Management
Mrs Isabella Beeton, 1861, www.
mrsbeeton.com

*The Butler's Guide To Clothes Care,
Managing the Table, Running the Home
and Other Graces*
Stanley Ager & Fiona St.Aubyn, 1980,
PAPERMAC

The Chronicles of Downton Abbey
Jessica Fellowes & Matthew Sturgis,
2012, Collins

*The Footman's Directory, And Butler's
Remembrancer*
Thomas Cosnett, 1825, Simpkin &
Marshall

*The Footman, Vol. XVI of the Industrial
Library*
1870, Houston & Sons

The Gentleman's Cellar & Butler's Guide
H.L.Feuerheerd, 1899, Chatto &
Windus

*The Housemaid: Her Duties and How to
Perform Them*
Houlston's Industrial Library No.20,
Houlston And Sons, 1877

*The Housekeeper's Guide to the use of
Preserved Meats, Fruits, Condiments,
Vegetables &c.*
Arthur Gay Payne, 1891, Frederick
Warne and Co.

The Lady's Maid: My Life in Service
Rosina Harrison, 2011, Ebury Press
(first published as *Rose: My Life in
Service*, 1975, Cassell & Company)

*The Servants Companion; Or Practical
Housemaid's and Footman's Guide*
William Bloomfield, 1860, J.R. Blonsell

The World of Downton Abbey
Jessica Fellowes, 2011, Collins

*Your Carriage, Madam! A Guide to Good
Posture*
Janet Lane, 1934, Chapman & Hall
Limited

www.stmartins.com

 ST. MARTIN'S GRIFFIN

175 Fifth Avenue, New York, N. Y. 10010
Printed in the United States of America